| DATE DUE | | |
|---|---|---|
| | | |
| | | |
| | | |
| | | |
| | | |
| | | |
| | | |
| | | |
| | | |
| | | |
| | | |
| | | |
| | | |

10376

# The Greeks

This book traces first the development of classical archaeology in Greece, from the antiquarianism of Renaissance scholars visiting Byzantine Greece to the large-scale excavations and studies of modern archaeologists of the Greek Archaeological Service and Archaeological Society and of the various foreign schools and institutes of archaeology in Greece.

An account of an excavation co-directed by the author describes what life is like on a dig in the hill country of Attica and the kind of museum work that has to be done to consolidate work in the field. Further chapters deal with the contribution of archaeology to our knowledge of how the ancient Greeks lived, with some recent archaeological achievements and problems, and with descriptions of individual finds and of a few great sites.

The author writes as one familiar with Greek sites, having some years' experience of fieldwork and excavation on the mainland and islands of Greece.

Cyflwynaf y llyfryn hwn i
Angharad, Rhodri a Chatrin
ac i ddisgyblion
Hen Ysgol Rad Llanrwst.

THE YOUNG ARCHAEOLOGIST BOOKS
*Edited by Robin Place, MA, FSA*

# The Greeks

WITH A FOREWORD BY
PROFESSOR HOMER A. THOMPSON

JOHN ELLIS JONES

*Maps and drawings by the Author*

G. P. Putnam's Sons   New York

ISBN 0 298 79123 4
Set in 12 pt. Lumitype Times
and printed in Great Britain

Published simultaneously by
Rupert Hart-Davis Educational Publications and
G. P. Putnam's Sons, 200 Madison Avenue, New York, N.Y. 10016
Library of Congress Catalog Card Number: 75–151223

# Contents

PROPER NAMES

Young archaeologists may find in their reading several forms of the same proper names of persons and places. It depends on whether an author transliterates the Greek name into English letters, or uses a familiar Latinized form—an ancient Roman adaptation of the name —or has adopted a transliteration of the modern Greek pronunciation. It is difficult to be wholly consistent, to reject familiar forms for unfamiliar transliterations, or again to create 'Roman versions' where no ancient ones are known. Common differences are Latin *c, ch, ae, i, u, -ium*, and *us* for Greek, *k, kh, ai, ei, ou, -ion* and *-os*. A few examples are:

**Persons:** Cleophon/Kleophon; Hercules/Herakles.
**Places:** Pentelicus/Pentelikos/Pendeli; Phaestus/Phaistos/Festos.

# List of Illustrations

# Foreword

Archaeology of the Classical Period has been overshadowed of late by glamorous developments in more exotic periods and places. This lively little book shows that interesting and important finds are still being made in Greece of the fifth and fourth centuries B.C., and that many problems relating to Greek life are still being solved by the enterprising archaeologist.

Based on sound scholarship and on much first-hand experience, the text is clear and fresh. Mr. Ellis Jones has succeeded admirably in conveying both the intellectual stimulus and the sheer pleasure of exploring a classical Greek site.

HOMER A. THOMPSON

Professor of Classical Archaeology,
Institute for Advanced Study, Princeton
Field Director, Excavation of the
Athenian Agora 1947–67

*May 18, 1971*

# CHAPTER ONE

# Archaeology in Greece

Two thousand four hundred years ago an ancient Greek named Thucydides, a citizen of Athens, in writing the history of the "Great War" of his age described the two most powerful states in Greece exactly as if he could see them with the eyes of an archaeologist of our own day:

> What if Sparta ever became a deserted site so that there remained only its temples and the leveled foundations of its buildings? I do believe that when a long time has gone by, future generations would find it hard to accept that Sparta's power ever matched the claims made for it. Yet today the Spartans own two-fifths of the Peloponnesus, and dominate the whole and control many allied states beyond its limits. Nonetheless, as they live, not in a single great city, but in the older Greek style, in a scatter of villages, posterity would be left with a very poor impression. Whereas if the same fate overtook Athens, the future would conclude from what is left to view that her power was twice as great as it really is today.

This book attempts to sketch what the archaeologists of the modern world have been able to make of the remains of the past, so as to re-create the realities of the age of Thucydides—the Classical Age. It was a great age and of enormous significance in the history of civilization. So it is fortunate that modern archaeologists do not depend on "looking only at the visible remains of cities"—against which Thucydides warns—but can use a wealth of evidence, including much of the writings of the ancient Greeks themselves.

Archaeology has come to mean the study of the material remains of the past, that is, the buildings and possessions of men long dead and the attempts to picture their life from these relics. The archaeologist may be able to study some remains above 9

A map of Greece. Places mentioned in the text are marked.

ground—the ruins of great buildings and objects still scattered around. He may have to search deeper and dig where he may know that remains lie buried, or almost at random, led by general clues. He must study and analyze his discoveries, measure and plan the buildings, collect and classify and date smaller objects. Finally, since all these researches are not purely an end in themselves, he should use these things (within the limits of the

10

material) to reconstruct what he can of the life of their former possessors. He must be capable of historical imagination. For the archaeologist, like many scholars in other fields, is concerned with the study of men.

For the greater part of the long story of man's existence—for the ages before men began to write, those before history—archaeology must be our main source of knowledge. We are bound to miss much. We shall probably rediscover only part, not all, of the material remains of the society that we set out to study. Again, we are limited to the physical, and then in practice usually to the imperishable possessions of that society. We may be totally ignorant of the nonphysical aspects of the people, of their thoughts, beliefs, and ideals, or only be able to make a guess at these by interpreting some of their practices. We may draw sound conclusions about the society as a whole or the changes in its customs over a period or even see the results of disasters that overtook it, but never know the names of its gods and its heroes, and the personalities and events of the day.

In such things prehistory remains stubbornly mute. The archaeologist realizes only too well how very true is that verse which the Roman poet Horace wrote so long ago:

> Vixere fortes ante Agamemnona
> Multi sed omnes illacrimabiles
> Urguentur, ignotique longa
> Nocte, carent quia vate sacro.

"Long before Agamemnon heroes lived, a host, but all have gone, without a tear, without a name, into time's long night: no Homer sang of them."

It is true that the archaeologist delving into the past, even into prehistory, need not work entirely alone. He can call on the support of experts in various sciences. The geologist and the ecologist may help him paint in the background of the physical world of his anonymous subject. The chemist, the metallurgist, the physicist, the electronics specialist, may analyze or examine in remarkable ways the objects he has found, and attribute them to their sources of origin and reveal much about their manufacture or their movement from place to place. But at times the pre-historian must long for the poet's aid.

Archaeology, however, is not confined to the prehistoric periods; it can serve equally well the study of the historical. In  11 these it is not the main, the only source, and to that extent it may be the less essential. But it can be all the more effective in combination with others. Archaeology can add an extra dimension to a distant age described for us by its own writers; it can illustrate a true record with examples of earthy reality; and it may check or correct a doubtful one. For the earlier phases of history, when the records are incomplete or uncertain, the contribution of the archaeologist may be the crucial one.

Prehistory has no fixed dates; it is a relative term. In some parts of the world one can extend the term to a period not so very long before our own, and the historical period is correspondingly shorter. For parts of northern Europe the history that depends on dates starts in the tenth century A.D., for the American continent from the fifteenth A.D. Yet elsewhere, as in parts of the Mediterranean and the Near East, dated history may be pushed back well beyond the tenth or fifteenth century B.C. To help them follow man's development in the long prehistory of northern Europe, the archaeologists of Scandinavia evolved the Three-Age System—the ages of Stone, of Bronze, and of Iron. These terms are relative. In parts of the Mediterranean the end of the Stone Age may be put in the third millenium B.C. (and may have covered the societies of walled cities as well as cavemen), whereas there are elsewhere in the world a few tribes still living today in their own local Stone Age. To follow man's development in any region entirely on the basis of such a system must be to describe it in general terms, with an inexact chronology. For the earliest periods archaeologists in Greece may need to depend on such generalities, but from a still early period they can work in terms of exact dates, known events, and famous personalities. They work side by side with the modern historian and literary scholar, and have the historians, dramatists, geographers, orators, and poets of antiquity as their allies.

*Classical* *archaeology*  The archaeologist who studies the Greeks is often called a classical archaeologist. The term "classical archaeology" is a wide one and can cover studies in any of the classical lands, in the homelands of the Greeks and the Romans as well, and the lands colonized, dominated, or influenced by them. But "classical" has another, more limited usage—that of a particular period of Greek history—and this book will concentrate on the

12  classical Greeks in that sense. We shall deal with the

The map shows the following labelled places: Olbia, CRIMEA, Chersonesos, BLACK SEA, Sinope, Odessos, THRACE, Byzantium, ASIA MINOR, PERSIAN EMPIRE, LYCIA, Rhodes, Salamis, CYPRUS, Epidaurus, ITALY, ILLYRIA, Massilia, Emborion, CORSICA, Alalia, Pyrgoi, Cumae, Tarentum, Epidamnus, EPIRUS, Metapontum, Croton, SPAIN, SICILY, Syracuse, Akragas, Gela, NUMIDIA, MEDITERRANEAN SEA, CRETE, Cyrene, Alexandria, LYBIA, EGYPT

archaeology of the Greeks, not from beginning to end, its prehistory as well as its historical periods, but with the archaeology of the Greeks of known ancient history.

A Map of Greek expansion.

*Greek expansion*

The Greeks of that period had settled and colonized the coastlands of much of the Mediterranean and the Black Sea. Since we cannot deal fully in a small book with the civilization of all these communities, a way of life so far-spread, let us concentrate on the ancient Greeks in their homeland, the areas where Greeks still live and the Greek language, descended from that of the ancients, is still spoken. Much of what is said can also be applied to these other areas. Greek literature and thought flourished there as well as at home, and architects—and simple jobbing builders—worked there too with equal effect. Some of the greatest Greek cities and finest examples of temples and theaters are to be seen in these other countries. But to these only passing references will be made, while a map of Greek colonial expansion will hint at the richness of material we must here overlook but about which you may be tempted to read further.

The names Greece and Greeks we have inherited from the Romans who applied the name of a particular group whom they met early in their contacts with the colonists in Italy, namely the 13

*Graii,* to the whole people. The terms used by the Greeks themselves, then and now, are "Hellas" and "Hellenes"—names which again had at first only a local usage in central Greece, as Thucydides tells us, but spread to the rest of Greece and to the Greeks wherever they went. From these names have been derived terms of convenience used by the archaeologist and historian, terms such as "Helladic," "Hellenic," and "Hellenistic."

*Greek pre-history*   By a convention Greek history may be said to have started in 776 B.C. This was the date of the first Olympiad, the first entry in the long list of victors in the Olympic Games. This was a record kept for nearly 1,000 years. It was used by the Greeks, for lack of a single common system of annual dating (like the B.C.–A.D. system of our Western world), as one useful Panhellenic chronology by which all Greeks could date, at least by 4-year periods. Before that, one might speak of the prehistory of Greece. Thanks to a century of archaeological discovery, that is no longer a long black night, a dark fog played upon by the uncertain light of ancient legends of heroes or modern speculation. Much has been discovered, the buried homes of the disembodied heroes have been unearthed, and prehistory's latter end we might call protohistory; we may not yet see the sharp outlines and clear light of history, but we glimpse the shimmer of its dawn.

Greece too has had its Stone, Bronze, and Iron ages, and the terms used include the more technical names of Palaeolithic, Mesolithic, and Neolithic for the old, middle, and new stone ages and Chalcolithic or Aeneolithic for the age of transition—the slow change from stone tools to those of copper and then of bronze. The term "Helladic" has been adopted to cover much of this prehistory of the mainland roughly from the Neolithic through to the end of the Bronze Age. Because archaeologists can distinguish many different phases of development within it, they divide the Helladic into Early, Middle, and Late Helladic periods (EH, MH, LH), each with numbered divisions and lettered subdivisions. So, they may refer to a particular phrase as Late Helladic III A or B or C and may be able to date it with approximate accuracy (but not always with unanimous agreement) to a century, a half century or less, within a decade or two. For the great island of Crete with its own remarkable prehistoric civilization, the term "Minoan" has been adopted (from

14

the name of the legendary King Minos of Knossos), again with its Early, Middle and Late (EM, MM, LM) periods and numbered and lettered divisions. Likewise, for the Aegean islands the term "Cycladic" has been adopted in the same way. Helladic, Minoan, and Cycladic phases are in general parallel with one another. For part of the late Helladic period the word "Mycenaean" is used in a chronological as well as a local sense, the term being derived from the great Peloponnesian citadel which was the most important center of this Bronze Age civilization—the Mycenae, "rich in gold," of Agamemnon of which Homer sang, as of some half forgotten heroic age before his own. This period has not left us a historical narrative, but is not entirely without some records—the archives of its palace store rooms, clay tablets inscribed with syllabic signs in the so-called earlier Linear A and the commoner Linear B systems, the second of which has been interpreted as adapted for a very early form of Greek. But all this wealth of archaeological material, this fascinating prehistory, deserves a volume of its own in this series.

The Bronze Age passed with the end of the second millennium into the Iron Age in a period of turmoil. Some of the great centers of Mycenaean power—royal citadels like Mycenae itself, Tiryns, and Pylos—were sacked and abandoned. Life became simpler in standards, more local, more limited. Historians have sometimes used the term "Dark Age" for this period, a term which should be understood to reflect perhaps as much our ignorance of the conditions of life then, as a primitive level at the time. Another term found is the "Age of Migration," for the Greeks of history had a tradition that refugee peoples flooded eastward from the threatened Mycenaean cities in the Peloponnesus, some settling for a while in Athens, others moving directly across the Aegean to settle the islands and the west coasts of Asia Minor. From this period developed the great age of Hellenic culture and the great historical age of ancient Greece.

The term "Hellenic" is not used much now in the semitechnical way that "Helladic" and "Hellenistic" are used, for it is possible to define the age more closely and to use a chronology of dates as well as descriptions. The earlier centuries, from the ninth to the sixth B.C., when dates may be only approximations, are frequently referred to by the use of general terms. These may relate to the development of architecture and sculpture, or the pottery motifs, or the literature, or the economic and political

*Historical periods*

15

organization of the period, so terms such as "Archaic" or "Geometric" may be used by archaeologists, or "Lyric Age" or "Age of Colonization" or "Age of Tyranny" by historians. With the great increase in historical records in the fifth and fourth centuries B.C., it is possible to discuss the material in stricter historical terms and to use close dates. These two centuries are pre-eminently the age referred to as the Classical Age, the great age of the city-states of Greece that created so much that was new in literature and thought—drama, history, oratory, philosophy, democracy—and bequeathed so much of all this to us to be part of the living heritage of Europe.

The end of the Classical Age can only be dated by the use of another convention. One may seize upon 322 B.C., the date of the deaths of Aristotle, the philosopher and Alexander's tutor, and of Alexander's adversary, Demosthenes, the orator of a free Athens, as a convenient date. It was Alexander the Great's career of conquest (336–323 B.C.) that marked the change from the classical world of independent city-states to that of great monarchies. His conquests and the new monarchies helped spread Greek patterns of life to areas hitherto little affected, to Hellenize the Near and Middle East and much of north Africa. There were many changes, largely for the worse, in this Greek civilization, especially in art. The new period is called the Hellenistic, and a convenient date for its end may be found in the Roman conquest of Greece and the destruction of Corinth in 146 B.C.

The changes that followed in the Roman period were mainly political—a further loss of freedom and initiative by the Greek cities. Culturally, however, the Greeks vanquished their victors, and this gave rise to a Graeco-Roman culture which spread all over the Roman Empire. This cultural unity in the Mediterranean lasted till the fourth century A.D. when it began to dissolve. The Roman era passed, gradually giving way to the medieval world of a feudal western Europe and a Byzantine Empire in the Greek East.

*City-states*    The civilization of ancient Greece was long-lasting, wealthy and complex, and, above all, urban. In Greek eyes it was the city that offered man the fullest life, a city independent and sovereign, where all the arts could reach perfection. This civilization has left a mass of material: great cities, some still lived in, others abandoned, their names and their sites forgotten; buildings in their thousands, some the pride of their age, most merely utilitarian; all the varied possessions in their millions, belonging to communities and individuals, products of master artists and of local handymen; writings and records, literary masterpieces and humdrum accounts. The great range of this material holds a variety of interests and calls for many specialized skills. Greek archaeology therefore embraces many branches of study.

One of the earliest to develop was **Topography**. This has involved the exploration of Greece, her islands, and the colonized lands, the rediscovery of long-lost sites and buildings, the identification of sites known by name, the preparation of maps of ancient Greece and detailed modern maps showing the ancient sites, and the whole study of ancient political and historical geography. The topographer may also examine the natural resources, changes in their nature, and their use in antiquity. These studies continue. Field surveys still reveal new sites hitherto overlooked, new details are annually added to our map of knowledge. Ancient authors are often our guides. Homer's "Catalog of Ships"—the list of cities sending contingents to Agamemnon's great expedition against Troy—has been used to identify many Mycenaean citadel sites in the southwest Peloponnesus in the 1960's, and now excavation at some has started. Strabo's geography listed cities and towns, demanding rediscovery. Pausanias' travel book helped the French archaeologists identify individual buildings and even statues at Delphi, the Germans likewise at Olympia, and helped American archaeologists name a building they have just found in 1970 on the north edge of the Agora, or market square, of Athens.

**Architecture** is another branch, and one which started early with the study of the standing ruins of temples so often shown in the drawings of early visitors to Greece. Ancient buildings in cities, towns, and religious shrines were often made of permanent materials—limestone or even marble—so many have survived as near-complete or as considerable ruins above ground, or have left traces recoverable by the spade. Not only do architectural studies include the detailed investigation of the fine and monumental examples—the ideal represented by the classical temple, with its various styles, its Doric, Ionic, and Corinthian orders—but also they cover other types of building, religious and secular, public and private, as individual forms and their grouping as elements in ancient town planning.

DORIC ORDER

IONIC ORDER

17

There is a close link between those studies and **Sculpture**. For the finer buildings, in particular the temples, were often decorated with sculpture in limestone or marble or terra-cotta, set upon the crests of their gable roofs or in the pediments, the low triangular spaces at either gable end, or below the eaves, as relief panels above the columns and lintel blocks, or as a continuous frieze along the tops of the walls. Other works again, molded in terra-cotta, carved in marble, cast in bronze, or plated in gold and ivory, were freestanding, intended to be set within buildings or in the open as religious dedications or as decorations in a public or private setting. Such studies can embrace the monumental and the miniature, taking in ivory carvings, statuettes, and the products of engraver, gem cutter, and goldsmith.

Many of these sculptured and molded objects were painted. But **Painting**, as a branch of Greek archaeology, suffers from a great lack of original large-scale examples. Master painters are known by their names; we read of paintings on wooden boards and frescoes on walls; we know of a Painted Portico at Athens, with pictures of famous battles, those between its hero-king Theseus and the Amazons, scenes of the Trojan War, and the battle of Marathon of 490 B.C. The Graeco-Roman frescoes of Pompeii in Italy give us some idea of late Greek styles and of the great loss occasioned by the destruction of earlier works. However, on the miniature level Greek painting is represented by a million examples on vases.

The study of pottery—**Ceramics**—considers both whole vases, sometimes found in excavated tombs undisturbed by collapse, and pottery found (as is more usual) in pieces, as potsherds. Sherds are the commonest finds on Greek sites, for, though they break again and scatter, they do not perish and, having no use or value, were not worth removing. Pottery studies form a vast field of their own with experts specializing in different periods. There are two main aspects. Fine glazed or painted pottery may be considered as an art form, reaching at times the level of great art. But pots, including the humbler, coarse, utilitarian varieties, may be studied as a key to chronology to give approximate dates. For, when a site has a long history of use, the older tends to be overlain by the newer, and layer upon layer of ruined buildings and floors and rubbish will be built up in what is called a stratified series. From the

18  datable objects found—dated coins and inscriptions—the

excavator may "read" the site's history from its own levels—which is the basis of stratigraphy. The pots and sherds will thus fall into a dated series, and other examples of the same class found elsewhere will be used to date levels at sites where perhaps no other datable objects may exist. Pottery changes its style in shape and surface decoration over the years, and so experts can classify and type and date potsherds on the basis of complete pots already studied. The terms they apply may be borrowed from the place of manufacture, from findspots, or from decorative styles. Examples are the very early Proto-geometric and Geometric styles (terms derived from the formal patterns of straight lines, curves, circles, and hatching, but applied in a general way to the period itself), Proto-Corinthian and Corinthian, Orientalizing (imitations of Near Eastern styles), Laconian, Rhodian, Melian, Attic, Black-figured (having human and animal figures painted in black glaze on the red fabric, left unglazed or reserved), and Red-figured (the opposite technique).

Another specialized branch is **Numismatics**, the study of coins and medallions. This is a complex subject since the Greek cities issued their own coinages with a great number of variant images (for Greek coins reflected politics and propaganda rather as modern postage stamps do). The numismatist may study coins as fine art, while the field archaeologist may be more concerned with their use for dating purposes.

Coins and vases, sculpture and buildings, often bear some words of Greek. Apart from these, thousands of marble slabs and bronze tablets were purposely set up in antiquity as records inscribed with a message for contemporaries or posterity. The study of inscriptions on durable materials, such as stone and metal, forms yet another branch: **Epigraphy**. Such records include epitaphs on tombstones, dedications on offerings made to gods or heroes, honorific publications of a patron's gift or a patriot's act, and documents recording public and private transactions, treaties, laws, decrees, contracts, accounts. The work of the epigraphist is to make transcripts of inscriptions, record them with photographs and molded impressions made of paper or latex rubber, study the forms of the letters, piece together fragments of texts; and publish his results. He may well throw light on the details of political life, date events, and rewrite history.

19

*Tinted amphorae*

Row 1—Attic Submycenaean, Protogeometric and Geometric (eleventh to tenth centuries B.C.). *Row 2*—Geometric and Orientalizing (tenth to seventh centuries); two Attic, Parian, Chalcidian. *Row 3*—Black-figured by Amasis, Mannerist Painter, Exekias (sixth century) and Red-figured by Berlin Painter (fifth century). *Row 4*—Three Panathenaic amphorae of sixth to fourth centuries (prizes at Athenian games); early Hellenistic vase of Athenian "West Slope" ware.

20

A branch closely allied to the last, but not much associated with discoveries in Greece itself, is **Papyrology**, the study of ancient papyri, or writings on paper. This was made from the Egyptian marsh plant *papyros* and was the usual writing material from classical times on. It is perishable and survives only in special conditions of dryness. Greece has produced only a fragment or two, Italy, Palestine, and Mesopotamia rather more, but the great mass of surviving papyri, counted in the

Inscription and papyros. Fragment of an Athenian inscription setting out contracts for the silver-mines of Laurium, fourth century B.C. Papyros fragments from Derveni near Salonika, a rare find from Greece.

thousands, came from Egypt—salvaged from tombs, deserted towns and villages in the rainless districts, or dug up in excavations such as the ones at Oxyrhyncus which recovered such a mass of manuscripts. The epigraphist can follow his interests in a great variety of material—public and private documents, letters, bills, lists, so much written only for the use of the moment but valuable as unself-conscious evidence of daily life, or again books and technical treatises or even works of literature, known or quite new.

These branches of study often overlap. It is certainly possible for scholars to devote themselves to one or the other in order to make new discoveries in their chosen field. But an archaeologist who intends to excavate must be aware of all; he may call on specialists to help on particular problems, but will need to know sufficient himself to be able to relate together and interpret all the evidence he may uncover.

Archaeology as a systematic study is a comparatively new development. True, we may find some fascinating examples of how the ancient Greeks themselves anticipated the approach of the archaeologist. We have already seen that Thucydides was able to speculate along archaeological lines. He even showed that he could interpret an excavation! For, in reviewing in a remarkably rational way the prehistory of Greece, he noted that the graves on the sacred isle of Delos were all opened and cleared to "purify" the place and that the weapons in most of them and the methods of burial indicated that they must have been those of Carian settlers, as proved by contemporary Carian practice in Asia Minor. The modern archaeologist could not have concluded differently, though he would have cataloged the small finds! The poet Hesiod described early times as a series of ages, starting romantically with ages of Gold and of Silver, and then speaking more realistically, as if fully aware of the conditions of life, of a Bronze Age before his own hard Iron Age. The historian Herodotus copied archaic inscriptions at Thebes and speculated on the Phoenician origin of the Greek alphabet, and a certain Philochorus edited a *Corpus of Attic Inscriptions* in the third century B.C. All this shows that some Greeks were curious about times before their own. However, the Greeks did not undertake that deliberate and systematic search for antiquities, their excavation, classification, and publication, which characterize archaeology proper.

It was in the last century that systematic archaeology really developed. Before that, there had been a long growth of antiquarian studies connected with Greece. Many explorers and collectors had prepared the ground. An outstanding example was the early-fifteenth-century traveler from Italy, Cyriaco of Ancona, who spent years traveling in Greece, copied inscriptions, identified the sacred site of Delphi, made drawings of the Parthenon—the great temple on the Acropolis of Athens—and collected (but did not publish) a mass of notes and sketches. But earlier the Western medieval world had shown little interest. The Byzantine Greeks, who had adapted old temples for churches, had been too familiar with ruins to be curious about them, and their gaze was on theology and eternity, not turned to the pagan past. The Turks who conquered them had even less concern; their long rule had a stifling effect on the Greeks and long hampered travel from the West. The Renaissance, that great revival of learning spreading from Italy over western Europe in the fifteenth and sixteenth centuries, stimulated the literary study of ancient Greek and, in time and indirectly, an interest in the land and its remains. Scholars began to penetrate Greek lands, as "cultural attachés" of embassies to Turkey or as agents or chaplains to trading companies in the Levant. Collectors and connoisseurs too saw in Greece an untapped source of *objets d'art*. The Earl of Arundel, the Duke of Buckingham, and King Charles I began a fashion in England in the 1620's by collecting sculptures for their galleries and gardens. Arundel employed as his agent the intrepid William Petty, who was not put off his searches by hard decks to sleep on, coarse fishermen's food to eat, imprisonment, or shipwreck, while the king even employed one of his admirals, Sir Kenelm Digby to rummage on Delos for statuary. Such private collections often became the nucleus of many a great modern national, civic, or university museum. Arundel's collection eventually went to Oxford; the "Closet of Curios" gathered by Tradescant, King Charles' gardener, was given to start the Ashmolean Museum, Oxford, in 1683; later the British Museum was founded in 1759 with Hans Sloane's collection of ancient coins and bronzes.

Topographical studies started as more travelers began to go to Greece, those from Britain playing the leading role but with others from France, Germany, and elsewhere also active. They

*History of Greek archaeology*

*Collectors*

23

Antiquarians in Athens. Nicholas Revett, James Stuart, James Dawkins, and Robert Wood viewing the Monument of Philopappos in Athens; from Stuart and Revett, *Antiquities of Athens*, III (1794).

*Topography* tramped or rode over the countryside; they sketched ruins, made notes, copied inscriptions, collected antiques, and wrote books of travel and descriptions of Greece. Notable for their time were the Englishman George Wheler and the Frenchman Jacques Spon; they made an archaeological tour together in 1675–76. They published books, Spon in 1678 and Wheler his *Journey into Greece* in 1682; both were considered standard works for a long time. When the French ambassador to Turkey visited Athens in 1674, artists accompanying him produced a series of drawing of the Acropolis and the Parthenon (the "Carrey" drawings) which are of great archaeological value as they show the state of the temple before it was wrecked by a terrible explosion in 1687.

Great advances in topographical and architectural studies came in the mid-eighteenth century. James Stuart—who had walked most of the way from London to Rome to study art!—
24 and Nicholas Revett spent three years, 1751–53, measuring and

drawing the monuments of Athens, and then (having escaped riots, plague, and murder attempts) returned to London to publish in 1762 the first volume of *The Antiquities of Athens*. The fine drawings, the first seen in England based on accurate measurements, made an impression; they brought Greek monuments before the eyes of armchair antiquarians. The Society of Dilettanti, formed in 1732 in London by noblemen and gentlemen with a taste for travel in classical lands and art collecting, had promoted these researches and financed others to come, such as Richard Chandler's Ionian Expedition of 1764 to Greece and Asia Minor which resulted in *Antiquities of Ionia* (1769, 1797), two volumes of inscriptions (1774), and two on topography, *Travels in Asia Minor* (1775) and *Travels in*

Recreating the past from pots. A selection of Thomas Hope's drawings of Greek costumes, from his *Costumes of the Ancients* (1812) re-issued in 1962 as *Costumes of the Greeks and Romans*.

25

*Greece* (1776). The dilettanti were patrons of taste, not archaeologists, but by supporting artists and architects they published accurate records, in superb volumes, of monuments since then damaged or lost.

The historical study of classical art was greatly advanced by the German J. J. Winckelman. His great *History of Art* (1764) sought to analyze the Greek approach, though it was based on Hellenistic and Roman statuary in Italy; the author probably never saw a Greek original of the classical period. The serious study of Greek vases was started by Sir William Hamilton, British minister to the kingdom of Naples (and husband of Nelson's Lady Emma). He made two collections of vases and other antiques found in Italy and Sicily and published them in illustrated volumes—the drawings inspired the still well-known Wedgwood ware. His vases were sold to the British Museum and to Thomas Hope, who showed how vase painting could be used to illustrate social aspects of classical times in his *Costume of the Ancients* (1812). *Art studies*

Travelers and topographers were very active everywhere in Greece and the Aegean coastlands in 1750–1820. Notable work was produced by Edward Dodwell, Sir William Gell, and, especially, William Martin Leake. Colonel Leake, a British military adviser to the Turks, surveyed Greece and Asia Minor and published detailed studies of lasting value, such as his *Topography of Athens and the Demes* (1821), *Travels in the Morea* (1830), and *Travels in Northern Greece* (1835).

Excavations were by no means unknown, but in this period were mainly directed at treasure hunting, the robbing of tombs for undamaged grave goods such as vases and ornaments, and the recovery of statues from ruined temples. The outstanding example of this approach was Lord Elgin's scoop in removing, between 1799 and 1803, and shipping off to London most of the surviving sculptures of the Parthenon and elements from other Acropolis buildings, all now in the British Museum. Similar in *Elgin marbles*

(*opposite*) The romance and reconstruction of antiquities. Reconstruction of the Parthenon (west end) by C. R. Cockerell, published in 1828, and a view of the actual state of the building a few years before the clearances; from H. W. Williams, *Select Views in Greece* (1829).

aim were the adventures of an international group, including the British architect C. R. Cockerell ("Grecian" Cockerell, who had a remarkable flair for drawn restorations of ancient monuments), the German baron Haller von Hallerstein, a Dane, and an Estonian. In 1811 they dug for and found the archaic sculpture from the temple of Aphaia on the isle of Aegina, now in the Munich Glyptothek, and in 1812 recovered the classical frieze (the "Phigalian Marbles") from the temple of Apollo at Bassae in the Peloponnesus, now in the British Museum. On another front, epigraphy had been advanced by various collections of inscriptions published in the eighteenth century, and a further step forward came when A. Boekh initiated in 1815 a plan for the Berlin Academy to publish a great new *Corpus Inscriptionum Graecarum.*

The Greek War of Independence (1821–28) held back all these activities in Greece for a time. The return of peace and the creation of an independent Greek state, now conscious of its great heritage from the ancient past, led to a great spurt forward. A French mission had shown the way in 1829 with excavations at Olympia and Epidaurus in the Peloponnesus. In 1833 a start was made on the clearing of debris and a jumble of medieval and Turkish houses and walls from the monuments on the Athenian Acropolis. The work was under the care of Greek enthusiasts and Bavarian architects and conservators appointed by the new regime of Otho I, who had come from Bavaria to be king of Greece. At last, the necessary public and private agencies for the systematic study and care of antiquities could be set up. State responsibility was recognized; the appointment in 1835 of a conservator of antiquities for the Acropolis was the start of the Greek Archaeological Service. There followed in 1837 the foundation of a Greek Archaeological Society and a university in Athens, in which the place of archaeology was recognized by the early appointment of a professor. Its recognition, likewise, as a university subject in Germany and France made possible systematic scholarship and a professional approach. The subject was slower to penetrate into the lecture courses at English and American universities; chairs in archaeology were created at London and Oxford only in 1880 and 1885.

The Greek state has generously welcomed the active participation of foreign scholars in excavation and research in Greece. Nothing did more to promote this than the foundation of foreign archaeological schools in Athens, to be research centers for scholars, architects, and graduate students from the founding countries, complete with fine libraries and their own hostels for their members. The French School of Archaeology was set up in 1846, an Athens branch of the German Archaeological Institute in 1874, the American School of Classical Studies in 1881, the British School of Archaeology in 1886, an Italian School in 1908, and a Swedish School in 1948.

These organizations financed and conducted some very large-scale excavations. The Greek Archaeological Society had already carried out some impressive clearing operations in Athens at the Odeion of Herodes Atticus in 1848 and 1857–1858, and a Prussian team dug at the Theater of Dionysus in 1862. But dramatic levels were reached with the personal excavations of Heinrich Schliemann, the German business tycoon turned archaeologist, at Troy in 1870–73 (and again in 1878–79) and at Mycenae in 1874–76, as later at Tiryns (1876, 1884–85) and Orchomenus (1880–81). These opened a new chapter in archaeology, revealing its possibilities for the pre-history of Greece and underlining the importance of stratigraphy and pottery dating. Such successes encouraged ambitious projects, and the complete excavation of the historic site of Olympia was planned by the German Archaeological Institute through its branch in Athens. The treaty between the Germans and Greek authorities laid down that all finds should remain in Greece (the export of antiquities was now understood to be a loss of the nation's heritage and was banned), but rights of first publication would rest with the excavators. From 1875 on, the Germans, under Dr. Ernst Curtius, his assistants, and successors, uncovered temples, shrines and a stadium, and discovered a famous named statue, the Hermes of Praxiteles, and a great store of archaic bronzes, which they displayed in a special museum built near the site. This encouraged the start of thorough excavations at several of the great religious centers. The French School dug at Delos from 1877 on, and at the oracle center of Apollo at Delphi from 1892 on. The Greek Archaeological Society, through such notable figures as Kavvadias, the national director of antiquities, worked at the healing shrine of Asclepius in Athens (1876–77), at the Asclepeion at Epidaurus (1881 on), at the center of the Mystery Cult at Eleusis (1882 on), at the shrine of

Amphiareus at Oropus (1884–87), and on the Acropolis of Athens (1885–87). The British School conducted excavations at Megalopolis (1890–91) and at Sparta (1906–10) and the American School at Corinth (1896 on). Ever since the discoveries of Schliemann and Dörpfeld at Mycenae and Tiryns, Tsountas in Thessaly and the Cycladic islands, the British at Melos, and in particular Sir Arthur Evans at Knossos in Crete, late in the last century and early in this, the Greeks and the foreign schools have given equal, indeed increasing, attention to preclassical sites.

*Greek Archaeological Service*    The situation today reflects these developments. The overall responsibility for antiquities, for the care of sites and repair of monuments, for rescue excavations, for museums and for supervision of all excavating agencies, lies with the Greek Archaeological Service. This is a government department, run by a Directorate of Antiquities and Restoration, part of the Prime Minister's Secretariat; its inspector-general is always a distinguished archaeological scholar. The country is divided into various regions with professional archaeologists in charge as ephors ("superintendents") of antiquities, assisted by epimeletes ("curators"), university graduates like themselves, and on a lower level by their museum or site staffs, called phylaces ("custodians"). Ephors and epimeletes may operate from one of the regional museums and will organize excavations and restorations and supervise any foreign expedition working in their area. They often direct also the research excavations financed by the Archaeological Society. Foreign archaeological schools finance and direct their own excavations, each being licensed

*Excavations*    normally by the authorities to work at three separate sites every year. But they may be given, over and above the usual three, extra permits to conduct emergency digs, or may excavate in formal cooperation with the Greek authorities (as a number of wealthy university expeditions have done). A school will often reserve one permit or more to continue work at one of its great traditional or long-lasting sites; so in recent years the Germans have often dug at Olympia and at the Ceramicus cemetery in Athens; the French at Delos and at the Minoan palace site of Mallia in Crete; the Italians at another such site, Phaistos, in Crete; the Americans at Corinth and at the Agora, or market-square, of ancient Athens; and the British at Knossos and 30 prehistoric Lefkandi on Euboea.

A great deal of Greek antiquities, small and not so small, *Museums*
are to be found in museums all over Europe and in America,
acquired through the avid collecting normal before the general
ban on this trade or by purchase since of licensed (and sometimes illicit) exports. The British Museum and the New York
Metropolitan Museum of Art, to name only two, have remarkably fine collections of statuary, bronzes, coins, and vases. In
Greece itself there are several museums. In Athens we find the
National Archaeological, the Epigraphical, the Acropolis, and
the Ceramicus museums for the prehistoric and classical, and
the Byzantine and Benaki for the medieval and modern periods.
There are excellent museums at Olympia (the richest collection
of archaic bronzes in the world), at Delphi, Corinth, Epidaurus,
Sparta, Heraklion in Crete (the best collection of Minoan art),
and Rhodes. There are museums in most cities and towns which
can boast an ancient site nearby, and indeed even in some
villages.

Discovery and display do not complete the archaeologist's *Publications*
task. Dissemination of knowledge is as important, and finds
have to be published. Many early excavations were never
described, or not described fully, so much knowledge has been
lost. Researches may be published as excavation reports, articles, and discussions in the periodicals of learned societies or as
monographs, that is, individual works which may vary from slim
essays on a single theme to huge volumes in a great series of
detailed publications of a single site or a great corpus or catalog
of bronzes, or coins, or vases. To enable scholars to keep up
with the pace of fieldwork, surveys of each year's excavations,
composed of summary reports, are included in several periodicals. The Greek Archaeological Service publishes an annual
*Archaiologikon Deltion* (in two parts, general "Studies" and
"Chronicles" or a survey of the kind mentioned) and *Analekta
Archaiologika ex Athenon,* a handbook of select brief reports
issued three times a year. The Greek Archaeological Society
issues its own periodical, *Archaiologiki Ephemeris*; its annual
transactions, *Praktika*; and its year's work, *Ergon*. The periodicals of the foreign schools include the French *Bulletin de corre-
spondance hellénique* (with its excellent survey, *Chronique des
fouilles*), the German Institute's general yearbook, *Jahrbuch*,
and *Athenische Mitteilungen,* and the Italian school's *Annuario*.
In English we have the *Annual of the British School at Athens* 31

and its *Archaeological Reports,* and the American School's *Hesperia,* while long articles on Greek archaeology often appear in the British *Journal of Hellenic Studies* and the *American Journal of Archaeology,* and briefer ones in the more popular quarterlies, the British *Antiquity* and American *Archaeology.*

So far we have gazed at the whole range of archaeology in Greece and have seen how these studies developed and how research is run today. But all has been in general terms. Let us now focus our eyes on one site and follow one excavation from its beginning to its end.

# CHAPTER TWO

# Hard at Work—on Site in Attica

Let us next choose one example of a recent excavation of a classical site in Greece. Let us see what archaeology can be like in the field, what work can be done on a site and afterward on the finds, and what may result from such studies. Many sites are very large and their history long and complicated. Excavation there may last several years and still only uncover part of the evidence. It is better for us to choose a small site and a simple dig, and to see it as a whole. We need a site where the work with pick and shovel, with trowel and brush, with acid and glue, with pencil and pen and book has been completed. Let us follow the excavation of a classical house in Attica, dug in the summer of 1966.

The house chosen lies all on its own some 12 miles south of *Situation* Athens in open country. It was therefore not part of a larger site and could be studied as a unit on its own. Its location was the far southern end of the mountain range of Hymettus, in a natural bowl in the foothills. The house was on the edge between mountain and farmland. It crowned a small rocky spur, covered like the high slopes behind it with aromatic shrubs and stunted pines, but almost encircled by plowland and with traces nearby of terraces used by farmers long ago.

The existence of this house was not unknown before its excavation. Some remains had always been visible on the ground. They had been identified as ancient before the end of the last century and marked as such on a map of the ancient sites of Attica prepared after a survey by German archaeologists led by the great Curtius of Olympia fame. There were other isolated sites in the same district, and as a Canadian scholar recently suggested in a description of them, they were probably farmhouses. The nearest village is that of Vari, a half-hour walk away, down on the coastal plain. That it was also the ancient center is suggested by the cemeteries excavated by Greek 33

Attica and the Vari site: maps and general view. The view is taken from below the Cave of Pan, looking down the mountain along the ridge to the site (*arrowed*); Vari is on the plain behind the wooded ridge on the right.

archaeologists along its edges; it may have been the center of the ancient deme, or parish, of Anagyrous. The nearest ancient site to ours is not another house but a cave which lies on the open mountain, a 20-minute walk uphill, an underground chamber entered by a narrow cleft in the ground. That site had been excavated 70 years ago by members of the American School of Classical Studies. It had been used in classical times, and slightly earlier, as a shrine of the god of nature, Pan, and his attendant nymphs, and of the god Apollo and the Graces; in regular use between the fifth and third centuries B.C., it had again been used, possibly once more for secret worship, in the fourth and fifth centuries A.D.

Let us move again downhill to our house. The visible remains were the four outer walls of the house, projecting from the ground as a row of boulders. On one side, the western, these foundations were high, even imposing, for the house rested there on a projecting terrace which its builders had raised to extend the level area. That terrace was more than a meter high at its freestanding south corner, and the outer wall resting on it was again close to a meter high. These walls were thick, built up of split boulders and great limestone slabs from the rocky site itself, set up on edge, and the core filled with rubble, built dry or with some earth in the filling. The only obvious traces inside were those of one square room with equally thick walls; it was set in the southwest corner above the highest point of the terrace. The rest was filled with earth and stones, and overgrown with shrubs and one or two small trees. But careful search of the ground in 1964 and 1965, carried out with an eye to future excavation, revealed a few other stones embedded where perhaps more rooms might be found. Again, outside the walls other lines of stones were now seen, perhaps the leveled remains of walls of an outer enclosure extending to the tip of the spur. *Surface remains*

With two friends I decided to seek permission to excavate this site because it offered a comparison with another classical farmhouse which we had excavated in 1960 elsewhere in Attica, north of Athens. Through our parent institute, the British School at Athens, we approached the archaeological authorities and the owners of the land, that is, the central Directorate of Antiquities and the regional Ephorate (Superintendency) of Antiquities for Attica, and then the Office for Ecclesiastical Property which administered the land for its owners, a monastery in Athens. *Excavation arrangements*

Permission was generously given to us to work under the authority of the ephor for Attica. He kindly allowed us to use his department's storage hut on a cemetery site at Vari for the temporary storage of our tools and finds, and arranged for the safe-keeping of the latter at the museum in Piraeus.

*Staff and workmen*

The staff of the dig consisted of John Graham, of Manchester University in England; Hugh Sackett, of Groton School, Massachusetts; and myself, from Bangor in Wales. There also came my wife, Renée, who cooked for the whole party; our two small children, Angharad and Rhodri, and a young Bangor student, Pamela Rhodes, who helped on the domestic side and acted as relief driver. Representing the ephor during the dig itself was Helen Theodoraki. We were helped by two specialists who paid us brief visits. Ken MacFadzean, of Glasgow University, who had acted as architect on several British School excavations, came one day with his surveying instruments to add details, such as levels, to the site plan we had prepared. Petros Petrakis, the British School's expert pot repairer, spent three days piecing together and repairing our better potsherds. We had as workmen for the first two weeks of intensive digging four skilled and stalwart Cretans, Michael Lambakis, Eleutheri Protogerakis, Emmanuel Blachakis, and Nikos Daskalakis. They had been trained in the long series of British digs at Knossos in Crete and had worked that summer for Hugh at another British dig on a Bronze Age site in Euboea. For a third week we hired two to four local workmen on a day-to-day basis.

*Finance and equipment*

What of the armaments for our campaign? First, the money. Our fighting fund was made up of grants from the British School itself, from the faculty of classics of Cambridge University, from Manchester University and the University College of North Wales. The staff paid the whole or part of their personal expenses. Heavier equipment—barrows, picks, spades, ranging poles—was loaned by the British School. Smaller items —*zembils* ("baskets" for removing earth), brushes, trowels, knives, bags, labels, pegs, and acid—were bought for the occasion. An estate car was hired to transport us and our baggage from Athens to Vari and for the daily trips from the village along the dusty roads to the site.

To establish a base, I rented a small house in Vari for 6 weeks. It had only one boxlike room, with an awning of reeds at the front and a smaller awning behind, converted with some

36

extra straw matting into a second bedroom. This had to accommodate five people and was used as dig headquarters and as the messroom, where all the staff and occasional visitors had their meals, breakfasting and dining in the cool of the day under the front awning and lunching away from the midday heat in the comparative cool of the enclosed room. Food for seven to ten people was cooked on a two-ring calor gas stove or cooled in an icebox fed with freezing blocks carried daily from the next village.

The excavation took place in July and August, 1966. The heat did not make it the most comfortable season to dig, but the long university vacation was the only time when we were all free. We had arrived in Athens in mid-July and spent a few days on preparations, such as making official calls, hiring the car, recruiting the workmen, buying equipment, and transferring all to Vari. And here also two or three days went on preliminary work. We had to make the storage hut ready for our work on the finds, clear a campsite nearby for the Cretan workmen, arrange and pay for a supply of water to be carried daily by a motorcycle truck to the hut, and transport the tools to the site.

All was ready. The campaign could open. We agreed with the *Fieldwork* Cretans on the hours of work: an 8-hour day, 6 days a week. Digging was to start at 6 in the morning on the site, and to continue with a half-hour breakfast break at 9 (*kolazó* was the welcome call) until the noon lunch break. So the day began for us with an early breakfast in the village at 5.30 a.m., a call at the storage hut to pick up the workmen and the waterjars (there was no modern source of water near the site), and a drive in the gray dawn along dirt tracks into the foothills. The early morning was cool, but the heat grew as the sun rose and the glare was intense. It was a relief to leave the site at noon; the workmen looked forward to a meal and a siesta under the pines, we to the cool of the house and a cold lunch. At 2, with refilled waterjars we all drove back for the afternoon's work. Two and a half hours later we returned, carrying empty jars as dry as their bearers, and full *zembils* of potsherds. After tea the staff worked on the finds, washing the sherds and sorting them into groups. When light gave out, about 8 in the evening, we gathered together at the house to dine out under the awning and to discuss the day's work and the morrow's plans, to the clink of wineglasses, the clatter of plates and the clucking of our neighbors' hens around our feet.

The first work on the site was to clear the interior of the house of scrub and loose stones so that our trenches could be laid out. The walls of the house defined a rectangle of about 13·7 by 17·5 meters. This area was subdivided with string and pegs into six smaller rectangular trenches separated by narrow strips or balks a meter wide. These balks would be used as pathways and barrow runs while the trenches were dug. Their vertical faces would also preserve a section from the modern surface through the earth overlying the floors and, where we dug deeper, down to the rock below. When the ground plan of the house had been revealed in the trenches, we could complete the picture by digging away the balks. We realized that the fill in the house—the earth and stones inside its walls—was not likely to be very deep, for the foundation walls broke the surface of the ground.

Each trench was given a code letter (A–F). As potsherds were separately collected from each trench, and from each new layer of earth, recognized as different by its texture and color, and again from each room or compartment found in a trench, the sherd baskets bore coded labels, with letters for trenches, Arabic numerals for levels, Roman numerals for rooms, and with the date added. Small finds were individually bagged and similarly listed and coded. This coding corresponded to the record made of each day's progress entered in our Day-Book. This was an excavation diary with descriptions and sketches, measured plans, lists of sherd baskets, small finds, and all the information which would be the basis for a final report on the work. John acted as recorder, and Hugh and myself directed the workmen, labeled the finds, and took measurements and photographs.

The plan of work for the first two weeks of digging (Mondays through Saturdays, July 25–30 and August 1–6) was to clear the interior of the house, trench by trench, following the order of the letters. This meant that the last trench dug would be the northwest corner, from which the excavated earth was barrowed out onto a spoil heap outside the house and its enclosure. The two most experienced workmen were pickmen, a third shovelled the earth, and the fourth trundled it away in barrows.

As we dug down we first removed the dark-brown surface soil. Below it we came to a thicker layer of redder earth which went on down to the floors of the house. This was the crumbled remains of the house walls. They had been built in a style that was (and still is) very common in Greece, of sun-dried mud

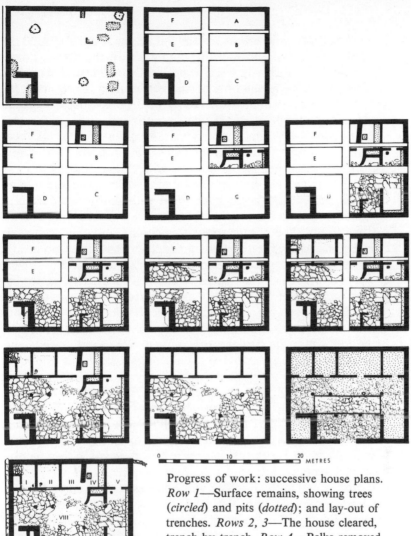

Progress of work: successive house plans.
*Row 1*—Surface remains, showing trees
(*circled*) and pits (*dotted*); and lay-out of
trenches. *Rows 2, 3*—The house cleared,
trench by trench. *Row 4*—Balks removed.
showing complete plan; plan omitting later
features, so close to the original lay-out;
plan showing roofed areas (*dotted*) with
paving restored. *Row 5*—Complete plan,
rooms numbered, and external terrace and
annex shown.

bricks raised on low foundation walls of rubble stone—the foundations which had remained as the only visible trace of the
house before our dig. This earth fill was not very deep, varying 39

from about 80 centimeters near the thickest walls to about 20 on the more open, exposed areas in the middle of the house. Small pieces of tile and sherds were scattered throughout. There was no clear trace of a build-up of successive floors; the main fill seemed to go down in most places to the original floors, and that suggested one single main period of occupation.

In trench A we found two rooms and about half of another, separated by two quite different walls. One was thin (30 centimeters) and built neatly but so low, with a level top, as to be a mere sill for the superstructure of mud brick. The other was much higher, wider, heavier, in build with crude boulder construction, as if it were a hasty afterthought. The rooms had earthen floors. The corner room was square and open, the next one narrow and cluttered with a bench of stones set alongside one wall and a very low platform of stones set near the other.

Trench B revealed the southern end of these rooms, closed by a long foundation wall, again neat, narrow and level-topped. There was a doorway into the corner room, and against the outside of the narrow room an odd earth-packed compartment with extension walls, one straight, one curved. We found close to the doorway a stone column base, left rough below but cut to a neat plain roundel on top; it seemed only to sit on the earthen floor. Further south, under a thinner cover of earth, were flagstones, much disturbed but clearly part of a paved courtyard.

Trench C disclosed more of the flagstone pavement, better preserved. It covered the whole trench, except for an earthen-floored room in the southeast corner, and ended with a neatly built edge against the room's west wall and along its open north end. Embedded in the flagging was another stone column base, a wider one with a round hole sunk in its center, as socket for a wooden column. Overlying the flags south of it was a poorly built and poorly preserved wall, suggesting that a corner of the court had been partitioned off.

The pavement ran on west into Trench D. In line with the embedded base was another hint of a colonnade, no stone base this time, but the round hole for one left in the pavement. But the main feature here was the corner room with the high thick walls that had been visible on the surface. These were like the outside walls of the house, more than twice as thick and three times as high as the sill-walls of the northern rooms. They suggested that the room might have been built higher than the rest, with upper

The Vari house after excavation: photographic view from northwest.

stories. We thought of it as our tower room, and its position on the highest corner of the terrace would have certainly added to the effect.

Trench E uncovered a further stretch of the paved court and an area of rock picked carefully down to give a natural floor on the same level. We also found the south ends of further rooms, a continuation of the façade found in trench B, partly founded on a rubble wall, partly on a shaped sill of natural rock. There were two doorways in it, one opening over a stone slab into a corner room, the other blocked with stones laid over its rock-cut threshold. Clearly some change of plan was indicated there.

The last trench, F, uncovered three rooms, two complete and part of a third already half uncovered in trench A. The corner room contained some strange features—two small compartments set against the west wall, an area of rough flagstones in the northwest corner, and a broken column base of the socket 41

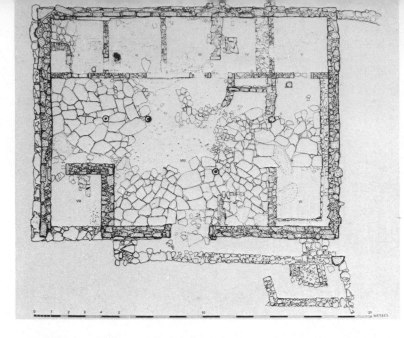

The Vari house: detailed plan of excavated remains.

type embedded on its side in ashy earth in the opposite corner. Most interesting was a group of complete or near-complete pots—two small bowls, a small pitcher, and the bottom of a wine jar—embedded high in the fill, not far below the modern surface; their condition and findspot suggested that they could date the abandonment of the house. The second room offered us some possibility of dating its construction: in a natural pothole in the rock we found another small group of scrappy sherds, buried beneath the floor of packed earth.

The last stage within the house was to remove the balks. Since the fill had been in places so thin and lacked significant layers, they had not revealed interesting sections. Their removal revealed far more. First, we could clear the entrance into the house, a south doorway wide enough for double doors. Then we found traces of a second row of columns along the north half of the court—two embedded stone column bases with sockets at the west and an emplacement for another at the far east end, revealed by part of a rounded hole in the flagstones and a circular depression cut in the rock below as a bedding. It looked as if the odd compartment in front of one of the north rooms and its two projecting walls had removed at least one, and probably two, such columns. It certainly blocked the clear run of a veranda along those five rooms.

42

Finding and repairing pots. *Above:* Michaelis digs out a group of pots in
room I, including a whole pitcher, seen just under his hand, and also on
right, and on the table below. *Below:* Petros at work in the storage-hut,
repairing pots, and an example of his work, a *kantharos* repaired, made-
up with plaster and tinted to match the black-glazed original.    43

Two weeks had been spent on clearing the house. The third week we spent on more intensive work on our finds, on measuring and planning the house.

*Work on finds*

The potsherds were cleaned as usual in Greece, well soaked in water and carefully brushed, and (to remove encrusted earth without damage to paint or glaze in particular) dipped in a weak solution of hydrochloric acid and soaked again in clear water. The sherds were spread on tables to dry, to be marked with the letter and number of trench and level, to be examined for possible joins, and to be grouped into types. Petros, the pot repairer, spent the latter end of this week with us. Using a calor-gas Bunsen burner and shellac, an adhesive softened by heat, he was able to piece together parts of a number of pots. The best was a two-handled cup of the "kantharos" type; the gaps left by missing sherds were filled with plaster of Paris and tinted. But few pots could be so treated. Our house was not a building suddenly destroyed with all its goods buried in the collapse, but one simply abandoned, ransacked perhaps, only its rubbish left and that dispersed by erosion. But we picked out for further study and preservation all fairly complete examples and all sherds which might help to date the house; that is, the few sherds with painted decoration and the plain black-glazed ones, the tableware of the classical period, and the more interesting fragments of unglazed coarse ware, the kitchen and dairy equipment. We chose fragments of rims, bases, handles, all pieces with an outline or shape allowing comparison with whole pots of similar profile whose date was known (*see illus. on page 43*).

*Exploration outside the house*

In a fourth week we resumed digging, this time outside the house with local men. We cleared the walls of the house and its surrounds of brush and rubble, and uncovered a broad step or veranda along its south face. At its east end was a small stone-built compartment, poorly preserved, enclosed in a small room or shed. That in turn was tied in with a larger enclosure partly surrounding the house. We explored and recorded the walls of this, clearing only the parts closest to the house. The enclosure had straight runs of wall and right-angled corners on its western and southern sides, but a more irregular and curving plan along the east, owing to the nature of the ground. The upper part seemed divided from the lower by a meandering wall which ran from near the shed across to the west side. The outermost walls

enclosed the tip of the spur, above the modern plowline, and bounded perhaps a garden on the slope in front of the house.

Other aspects of our work at Vari I can only mention briefly. Sundays were a break, but not a rest; we visited some other house sites in Attica, some excavated, some only described by others, in the hope of noting points of useful comparison. We, too, had visitors at our site. One day we benefited from the visit of Professor Homer Thompson, then director of the American excavations in the Athenian Agora, and from his comments on oddities of the house plan and our collection of potsherds. Our last few days at Vari were spent in making final records, tidying up the site, protecting the remains with a cover of earth, and returning our tools to store at Athens and boxing our finds for transfer to the museum at Piraeus.

But the end of a dig is only the start of other studies. Hugh had to return to America before long, but John and I became Athenian commuters for the rest of the summer, traveling daily by bus or train from Athens to the Piraeus to study our finds. These were not works of art, but simply a few oddments, three or four coins, and the broken crockery of an ordinary household, mostly coarse ware. From such rejects and remnants we had to re-create history. *Museum studies*

We settled down in the museum storeroom to identify each type of pot, to measure the sherds, calculating the diameter of rim and base from the curve of the piece left (matching each with a chart of concentric circles), and to write full notes for our catalog of pots. Then we would try to match our sherds with better examples of the same type of pot, illustrated in excavation reports or some great catalog or corpus of pottery collections, or noted by us during patient viewing of row upon row of pots in museums. So our mornings and afternoons we spent at our table in the Piraeus, our evenings at the desks in the library of the British School at Athens. Some days we passed in the museum of the Stoa of Attalus in the Agora of Athens, an ancient building rebuilt by American benefactors to preserve all the finds from the Agora excavations and now a treasury and powerhouse of archaeological knowledge. On its upper floor we could spot parallels in the pottery collection in glazed cabinets, look them up in the vast card index of pots, and in the basement search for others among the repaired pots stacked from floor to ceiling on open shelves.

We had spent two busy months hard at work, and much still 45

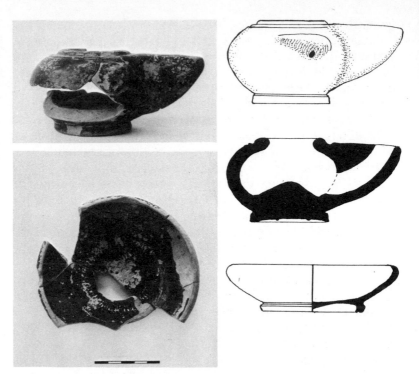

Potsherds and profiles. Photographs of a black-glazed oil-lamp and shallow bowl, repaired from fragments. Drawing showing external and sectional views.

remained to be done. But our other work called us home. Before we left, we submitted summary reports and photographs to the director of our school and the ephor of Attica and the heads of other institutes for inclusion in the annual reports and reviews of excavations published by them.

*Pot drawing*

In the summer of 1967, when we returned from excavations at Knossos, Hugh and I had a chance to work together on the Vari material. The pressing need was to prepare scale drawings of all the pots to be published. So once again, for 3 weeks, I adopted the routine of commuting, of 8 hours' poring over sherds with pencil and dividers in hand, of lunching at waterside cafés at the Piraeus, of evenings in the school library and stolen hours in the Agora collection. Two things were done. The catalog notes were redrafted, and a sheaf of pencil drawings on graph paper prepared. The usual convention was followed, of restoring the profile of the pot (where possible) on a fixed scale, at full or half-size, and drawing a cross section of the pot on one side of the center line and an outer view on the other.

46

Regrouped, retraced in ink and reduced in size, these would become black and white figures in our final report. Hugh was free to join in the final checking of catalog and drawings and to take some close-up photographs.

It seemed that the practical work was finished and that we *Beehive pots* could confine ourselves to our studies and libraries, to write our report on the basis of all our notes and drawings. But a new approach was called for when we considered closely one special type of pottery of which we had very many examples as sherds. These were large coarse pots (like very large, deep flower pots) with about half their inner surface grooved and scratched from top to bottom and side to side as if with a comb. Apparently belonging to this group were rings of similar fabric (like giant napkin rings), also combed around their inner surface, and flat lids with irregular patterns of ridges and small holes and a half-moon indent in one side. A few examples found at other sites had not been satisfactorily explained. But we had seen repaired, unpublished examples in 1966 in a private collection in Attica. The owner, Ioannis Geroulanos, had suggested such pots were

Beehives ancient and modern. Sketch and photograph combined, to show two views of a reconstructed ancient beehive from Trachones, Attica, with pot-hive, extension ring, and lid held together by a stick and cords, and a modern parallel from the islands.

terra-cotta beehives and lids, to be set horizontally in terrace walls like the modern (but "uncombed") examples in recent use on some Greek islands; set thus, the combing on the roofs of the ancient examples would be intended for the secure attachment of the hanging honeycombs, and the rings, slipped between pot and lid, would aid the removal of harvested combs (like the detachable stories, or ekes, of modern box beehives).

In 1969 John and a scientific colleague, Dr. Bu'lock of Manchester, conceived a method to test for minute traces of beeswax on our combed ware; the sherds would be soaked in a special solvent. This would evaporate, and its sediment could be submitted to scrutiny in electronic equipment. That summer, at the close of excavations elsewhere in Greece, I was able, with the kind cooperation of the museum authorities and many Greek friends and the active help of Dr. Bellos, a chemist at the Athens Polytechnic University, to prepare in the Piraeus museum and in a laboratory at the Polytechnic the necessary samples for examination at Manchester.

*Publication*   The final task of the archaeologist is to publish a report on his work. An excavation unpublished is not only no gain in knowledge (apart from the excavator's own, which dies with him) but a positive destruction of knowledge. Digging is after all a form of destruction, since it disturbs the evidence which others might have looked at. So for them the excavator must write a full account of his work and of the remains, and put forward his conclusions. In the case of the Vari house excavations, brief advance notices have already appeared, in Greek, British and French journals, and the full report will appear in the *Annual of the British School at Athens* (Vol. 67, 1972). Here only a summary is attempted.

*Description*   The house was a freestanding building, facing south and *of the house*   opening into its own outer yard or garden. In general character it was of a common Greek and Mediterranean type, a courtyard house, with its rooms grouped around an internal court. It was well laid out as a rectangle in a proportion of 4:3. Regularity like this was convenient for the builder and was possible on a free site uncluttered by other houses. But building a house here astride a ridge involved the effort of raising a terrace at the ends and leveling the rock in the middle.

The house was of a good size, but not outstandingly large.
Measuring about 60 by 45 Greek feet, it had three-quarters of

the area of the standard house plot of 60 by 60 feet in the "modern quarter" of the city of Olynthus in northern Greece, built up and occupied about 430–350 B.C.

Like most Greek houses, it used the materials ready at hand. Here these were local limestone for the foundations, mud bricks for the walls (probably limewashed to render them waterproof), packed earth for the floors of rooms, limestone flags for the open court, timber for doors, window frames and shutters, and roof beams, and kiln-baked tiles (of the large concave variety called Laconian) for the roofing, glazed with streaky red-to-black paint to shed the rain better.

The plan included a block of rooms (I–V) along the north side (five in all as seen from the excavated remains, but perhaps four originally), two more rooms in the southern corners (VI, VII), and a large flagged courtyard (VIII). The court had been enclosed and shaded in part by colonnades, probably two, one a full-length portico fronting the north rooms, with a return at each end to join onto the south corner rooms, and then a second, shorter portico between these. We have already noted some hints of slight changes of plan during the life of the house, structural additions and degeneration. As examples we have the reused column base in room I, the blocked doorway in room II, the clumsy partition wall between rooms III and IV, the projecting compartment or base in front of room IV blocking the north portico, and the extra room or shed built over the flagstones just west of room VI.

With regard to the probable elevation of the house—its appearance as it stood on its foundations—we must take the variation in the breadth and height of the walls as our clue. The outer are thick and high as if for extra strength and security, most of the inner low and slight (and that hardly for lack of material) and probably too thin to bear great weight. We conclude that the rooms were low, with no upper story over rooms I–VI and no gallery over the porticoes. But by the same indication, the walls of room VII were strong enough to bear probably two upper stories—a kind of tower.

Gathering the evidence together, I have sketched a reconstruction and made a small model. No certainty is claimed, but these give a reasonable impression of the house as it might have been when lived in twenty-three centuries ago.

Some interesting parallels can be drawn from ancient literature    49

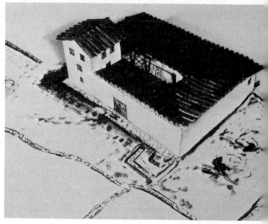

Reconstruction views of the Vari house.
*Top:* the house from the west, showing
towered building, garden enclosure and
terraced slopes. *Above and left:*
drawings and model.

and from other excavations. The Athenian writer Xenophon (*ca.* 430–354 B.C. once described a proper house as facing south, with a portico (*pastas* is his word for it) so sited as to trap the low rays of the winter sun and to give shade from the high sun of summer. American archaeologists who excavated at Olynthus in the 1930's recognized there classical houses built on that principle with the living rooms on the north side (with bedrooms overhead); a wide portico or corridor room in front of them; and a courtyard in front of that, flanked by other side rooms. They called this the *pastas* type of house. Demosthenes, again, the great Athenian orator (384–322 B.C.), in a speech about an "assault and battery" case, described a farmhouse, somewhere in the suburbs of the Piraeus, as having a tower (a *pyrgos*) in which the women servants locked themselves for safety when the house was ransacked. The Olynthus houses had no towers, but freestanding "towers" have been identified as unexcavated farmhouses or industrial compounds near Sounion (those visited in 1966) and as detached elements in loosely planned town houses at the Greek colony of Colophon in Asia Minor. One interesting result of the Vari dig is that we seem to have a house with a tower, a *pyrgos*, as an integral part of a well-knit *pastas* type of house.

For the history of the site we depend entirely on our finds; no mention of this farmhouse can be found in ancient Greek literature! The bulk of the pottery is dated by parallels to the end of the classical period and the beginning of the Hellenistic, to the late fourth and early third centuries, say 330–280 B.C. The date is supported by three bronze Athenian coins of the same period, one with the pig symbol of the Attic town of Eleusis. A few earlier sherds of the fifth century B.C. (in particular a few in the pothole in room II) suggested some earlier activity on the site, but too early to be related to this house. The abandonment is dated by the whole pots in room I, which are of the same date as the bulk of the sherds, without any particular late feature. This supports other hints—such as the absence of heavy wear on the raised stone threshold of room I—that occupation was not very prolonged, perhaps a generation, two at most. The end was undramatic. The house was not burned, simply abandoned and left to rot, or perhaps, since the household articles were so few and the tile fragments so very small, first dismantled and ransacked for anything which could be used elsewhere. At various 51 times, much later, people reused the site, perhaps to camp during harvests or to build a hut in the decayed ruins. We found some scraps of oil lamps of the fifth century A.D. (which might fit in with the second period of visitation to the cave of Pan on the hill above) and scraps of medieval Byzantine yellow-glazed bowls and gritty cook pots, together with a coin of the emperor Alexius I (A.D. 1081–1118).

The sorry remains on the site represent what was once a home, probably for an ordinary family. Men and women lived there, probably children too. Since they left so little behind, we have only an inkling of the life they led. But we can imagine some aspects: the family at meals when we look at the black-glazed bowls and plates, the husband quenching his thirst when we lift the kantharos, or pitcher, the wife cooking or spinning wool when we handle the fire-stained casseroles or the solitary spindle whorl found, and we may visualize a child playing as we turn to the one miniature piece, a delicate saucer the size of an infant's palm—children even then must have had their toy tea sets.

And what did these people live on? The products of the land surely. Where now a tractor had ripped open the earth around the ridge, an ancient farmer might have hoed his stony field to raise a crop of beans or barley or to establish his vines or olives. The tinkling bells of flocks reminded us that on the thin cover of the slopes around he would have pastured his sheep and goats. The liquid honey that we spread daily on our bread at Vari and the pitiful scraps of our farmer's beehives recalled to us the fame of Hymettus beeswax and honey; these might have been the other harvests of the slow rhythm of his work and days.

# CHAPTER THREE

# Light on the Past

We have considered the excavation of one site, a Greek house, the home of a forgotten family. The remains gave us the setting for their private lives, but little else, for so few of their personal belongings were found. We are still left rather in the dark as to what Greeks wore, what and how they ate, and what they did for a living. To see how archaeology can help us, we shall look at just a few aspects of private life and consider what light has been thrown on them by excavators elsewhere and experts in various fields. Naturally we have to deal with the material and physical aspects of life, not because they are necessarily the most interesting and worthwhile things to know about the Greeks (for their literature and thought rank higher), but because such is the stuff of archaeology, the evidence of durable materials.

Let us start with what is nearest to a person, his clothes. Old *Ancient dress* clothes are not what people treasure nor what we expect to survive for centuries. It is true that in certain exceptionally wet or dry conditions fabrics can last indefinitely, as is shown by woolen smocks and breeches recovered from long-dead bodies preserved in Irish or Danish peat bogs and by linen dresses and sheets from deep tombs or naturally arid sites in Egypt and Mesopotamia. But such conditions are very rare in Greece, and only a few fragments of cloth have been recovered, one actually in Koropi, the next village northeast of Vari, found in a bronze vase. It was a costly linen cloth, embroidered with silver-gilt thread in a trellis pattern with a tiny lion in each "diamond." Its date was the late fifth century B.C.

Since we have so few samples of cloth and none of clothing, our direct evidence is limited to costume jewelry. Remarkable specimens of gold and silver jewelry survive—rings, bracelets, necklaces, earrings, and coronets—but these only add to the total effect of costume. Dress fasteners are more helpful. Very 53 striking are the pairs of long decorated bronze pins found in some Dark Age graves which contain burials rather than cremation urns. The pins are found above the collarbones of the skeleton, one on either side of the neck. The gown that they fastened at the shoulder had perished, but the pins remained in place. They hint at the early date and wide distribution of a form of dress which became very common in archaic and classical times, and their size suggests a heavy material, wool rather than anything gauzy.

*Costume in art* Representations of costume in art, in sculpture, statuettes and vase painting fill in this meager evidence. The human figure in costume had appeared in Minoan and Mycenaean art, so we have a clear impression of the flounced skirts and tight bodices of the ladies and belted loincloths of the men. But the motif nearly disappears from Dark Age art, being reduced to stylized forms such as silhouettes and matchstick men. However, in archaic and classical art the human form and costume once more became emphasized and ever more accurately shown.

Sculpture has effectively recorded the drapery and details of women's costumes. Early sixth-century statues from Samos illustrate a costume consisting of a long tunic falling in tight folds to the feet with a wrap over it. A group of later sixth-century female statues, called *korai* ("maidens"), found on the Acropolis of Athens in two exciting days of discovery in February, 1886, show again the same fine crinkled tunic and mantle, now with rather heavier, elaborate folds, arranged diagonally across the front of the body as if supported by a sling. Several bear traces of paint, one having a greenish tunic and a paler (unpainted) mantle with patterned border and scattered rosettes in dark red. The paint on robes, hair, eyes, and lips, intended to enliven the pale cream of the marble, was remarkably preserved because the statues, perhaps protected from the weather when in position, had been buried with rubble used to fill cavities on the Acropolis in the clearance carried out soon after the Persian sack of Athens in 480 B.C.

In the same Acropolis group was a *kore* wearing a different type of dress, a fairly tight gown of heavier and stiffer material worn folded around the body with a deep overhang, like a sailor's collar, at front and rear. This statue, dated about 540 B.C. may be compared with two reliefs of about 460 B.C., one from the Acropolis of Athens and the other from the temple

*Korai* and caryatid: dress in stone. *Above:* two
*korai* from Samos (570–550 B.C.) and two from the
Athenian Acropolis (*ca.* 535–525 B.C.). *Below:*
Athena on a metope from the Zeus temple,
Olympia, and on the 'Mourning Athena' stele in
Athens (*ca.* 460 B.C.), and a caryatid from the
Erechtheum, Athens (*ca.* 415 B.C.).

55

Female dress:
fashion sketches.

Doric *peplos*

Ionic *chiton*

*Himation*

of Zeus at Olympia. Both represent the goddess Athena wearing the same type of dress, but rather fuller with softer folds and a longer overhang, which in one case is constricted within a girdle, in the other hangs free outside it.

Literary references help us identify these two styles. The historian Herodotus, writing in the mid-fifth century B.C., tells a story about a change of fashion taking place in Attica some generations earlier. He relates how the women, in fury at the loss of their own menfolk in battle, stabbed the sole survivor to death with the long shoulder pins of their dresses (obviously deadlier even than Victorian hat pins!); and so were made to give up the Dorian style universal till then, and adopt the lighter pinless linen tunic of the Ionic kind, so called from being already in common use among their Ionian kinfolk in Asia Minor. We conclude that the Dorian dress must be linked with the long pins found in early graves and that it was a woolen gown, and that the Ionic is the other style with thinner tunic and overwrap. From this and other such accounts scholars have revived the term *peplos* for the woolen gown, *chiton* for the tunic, and *himation* for the mantle.

But sculpture disproves one part of the story. The Ionic did not entirely replace the Doric dress in Attica, for both styles appear together on gravestones of the late fifth century B.C. and on the monumental frieze of the Parthenon showing Athenian ladies in procession. But certainly the overlong pins disappeared there, replaced by neater (and less dangerous) brooches.

Statuettes of Hellenistic times, found in great numbers at Tanagra in central Greece, illustrate also the larger over-mantles and flat hats that women adopted for outdoor use. Vase paintings again show us the whole range of dress and scenes of women putting on the various types. They make it clear that the *peplos, chiton,* and *himation* were really only lengths of cloth straight from the loom, draped and folded, pinned, stitched, and girdled in a limited variety of ways. It is then possible to reconstruct the form and the manner of wearing these dresses.

The same kind of evidence illustrates the costumes of Greek men. These too were simple, stable in fashion, and similar to women's dress in basic form and make-up; indeed some items of men and women's dress were interchangeable. With these illustrations and various references in ancient authors, we can identify most forms: the workaday *exomis,* a knee-length tunic

56

fastened on the left shoulder leaving the right bare; the *chiton* fastened on both shoulders; the *xystis,* the longer formal tunic; the *himation,* the outer mantle worn sometimes as the sole garment; the *chlamys,* the soldier and traveler's half cloak pinned at throat or shoulder and worn perhaps with sandals or half boots, *embades*; and a tall felt *pilos* or the *petasos,* a low broad-brimmed felt or straw sunhat.

In contrast to these soft costumes, one class is almost as well *Armor* represented by surviving specimens as by representations, and that is armor, particularly bronze armor; bronze corrodes, but much less readily than iron. Bronze armor goes well back into Mycenaean times, and Homer and other poets dwelt on the magnificence of the princely armor of the old heroes. Odd fragments have survived, such as a bronze helmet with cheekpieces from Knossos, dated about 1400 B.C. But by far the most impressive single find was the complete suit of body armor, almost miraculously preserved, recovered during Swedish excavations at Dendra, ten miles from Mycenae, in 1960. It lay together with bronze objects, including cheekpieces for a leather helmet, fragmentary greaves, and cheekpieces and boars' tusks from another helmet, in a grave dated again about 1400 B.C. The suit, made from several plates of bronze fitted together, covered the body from chin to knee.

Armor of the archaic and classical periods did not usually cover the body so fully, and the warrior's full defensive armor, his panoply, might consist, apart from shield and "clip-on" knee-length greaves for the shins, of only cuirass and helmet. French excavators at Argos in 1953 found in a warrior's grave of the late eighth century B.C. a magnificent suit of just these two items, a cuirass of the bell type, so called from its shape with outturned lip at waist and its lightly molded, formalized pattern suggesting muscles, and a helmet, conical with cheekguards and a curved crest holder (for horsehair or feathers) set on a tubular stem. The Dendra and Argos suits, both to be seen in the Argos museum, offer an interesting comparison between Greek armors separated in time by seven centuries.

The richest collection ever of archaic bronze armor resulted from the German Institute's excavations of the stadium at Olympia in the late 1930's, 1950's, and 1960's. The finds were mainly discarded war trophies and personal dedications; one helmet bore the name of Miltiades who led the Athenians to 57 victory over the Persians at Marathon in 490 B.C. They included not only several cuirasses, variously shaped helmets, knee-length greaves and shields, but pieces sometimes used in the sixth-century panoply but omitted thereafter to gain mobility—items such as upper-arm and forearm guards, thigh guards and spats for ankle and instep. Other forms of armor suggest various local developments; Crete, for example, has produced several semicircular aprons (the so-called *mitra*) probably used hanging just below the breastplate.

Most of the Olympia cuirasses were of archaic bell form, waist-length with stylized modeling and decoration. But some specimens found elsewhere, notably in Italy, illustrate a later development; the muscled cuirass, a fifth- and fourth-century type with longer breastplate curving down over the stomach and realistically molded to the form of a heroic torso.

Helmets have survived in fair number, of various styles and periods. They show that different types were in use, some perhaps commoner in certain regions than others, that improvements were made within types, and that some forms of helmets were ousted by newer ones in time.

Sculpture, statuettes, and vase paintings add their own information. They show various forms of crests which can only be deduced from ridges and hooks on real helmets, and portray arm and thigh guards—rare parts of a panoply, rarer still as survivals. They also show us a type of cuirass of which we have not even one actual specimen. That in itself is negative evidence that this corselet was of perishable material, and vase paintings of warriors arming add positive proof. The wearer dons it by pulling round his ribs a kind of corset which fastens down the front or side, ends at its lower edge in flaps, and has fixed at the back broad straps that stick up behind the shoulders and are then pulled down over them and fastened at the front. Clearly the material is pliable, as if the basic form were a leather (or fabric) jerkin. Some are shown plain, others faced in parts with scales or small plates (and bronze scales found at Olympia and Delphi could have been so used), or reinforced with a stiffer panel or plate in front. Furthermore, the art forms, since they can be dated on style, will suggest how armor developed over the years and when fashions changed, as from the archaic bell cuirass to the classical composite corselet or muscled cuirass.

Finally, literary evidence in plenty will give us the terms used

(a)

(b)

58

for individual parts of the military costume, such as *kranos* (helmet), *thorax* (cuirass), *knemides* (greaves), and *parameridia* (thigh guards), and some names of particular types, such as Corinthian and Boeotian for varieties of helmets (which the modern scholar has identified, naming others by other regional names used as terms of convenience, such as "Illyrian," "Chalcidian," "Attic," and "Thracian"). Also, there is no lack of information about the importance, use, and advantages of all this costly equipment, for war was part of the whole way of life. Our Vari farmer, if a full citizen with the right property qualification to serve as hoplite, or heavy infantryman, might well have had his own panoply hanging up on the wall in his house (*see illus. on page 62*).

From the costumes that Greeks wore round their bodies, we move to consider the roofs they raised over their heads. We have already looked at one Greek house standing on its own. So let us now look at houses in the mass. The largest continuous extent of ancient houses excavated in Greece itself is to be found in the Chalcidice peninsula in northern Greece, at Olynthus. This site was excavated in 1928–38 by an American university expedition working through the American School, and the results were published in a magnificent series of volumes. The place had been abandoned centuries ago and was no longer known by its ancient name, but it was reidentified by the excavators and its history rewritten from their discoveries and the ancient references to the historical Olynthus.

The city occupied two steep-sided but flat-topped hills near the mouth of a river, controlling a large tract of coastal plain. One hill had been briefly occupied by Neolithic farmers, reoccupied in the Iron Age, sacked by the Persians (479 B.C.), colonized by the Greeks, Chalcidians from Euboea, and later chosen as the center for the Chalcidian League, a breakaway state formed by the Greeks of this region after their revolt from the Athenian Empire in 432 B.C. The hilltop town became a city with a much bigger population, so a great extension was planned, spreading from the original hill town (on the South Hill) north to another broader plateau (North Hill), over the dip in between and the gentler east flanks of the hills, and eastwards onto the plain.

This new city is a wonderful example of Greek town planning based on a grid of streets, the type called Hippodamian after Hippodamus, of Miletus, who had introduced the system from

(c)

(d)

(e)

Body armor: surviving specimens

(a) Dendra suit

(b) Argos suit

(c) "Bell-cuirass"

(d) Mitra

(e) Muscled cuirass

59

"Cretan"

"Chalcidian"

"Illyrian"

"Corinthian"

"Thracian"

"Boetian"

Types of helmets
(*see page 58*)

Asia Minor to Greece a few years earlier. On the North Hill, the most fully explored area, the grid is based on north–south avenues 5 and 7 meters wide and east–west streets again 5 meters broad. These define at least eighteen blocks of about 35 by 86 meters, or an intended 120 by 300 Greek feet (on the shorter foot standard of Euboea, from where the first settlers came), and other blocks of 120 feet square. The long blocks contained ten houses, in two rows of five separated by a narrow drainage alley. The standard house plot was 60 feet square, but was reduced in practice, by loss of space to the alley and by the overall shortening of some of the blocks, to something like 58 feet square (*see illus. on pages 63 and 65*).

The Olynthian houses were of great interest, for their excavation threw new light on classical houses on the mainland. As houses in a block have party walls and bonded foundations, it seems that all ten were built at the same time, probably with their upper floors and roofs at a common level. But unlike the house blocks of so many nineteenth-century industrial towns of England and twentieth-century housing estates, the individual houses in Olynthian blocks did not have identical plans; indeed, no two are quite the same. However, they are of one basic type, variations upon one theme, whether they are the commoner square houses of the North Hill or the broader-fronted houses on its eastern edges. Each is a courtyard house, with the court on the south and a roofed block on the north, and extra rooms on either side of the court. The main roofed block contains three to five living rooms along the north wall and a long corridor room opening through piers, columns or over half walls into the court. This portico, or *pastas,* has given its name to this house type. The portico sometimes extended around other sides of the court, giving rise in a few cases to the full peristyle court—the all-round portico type. The street door led into the court, directly where the houses stood on the south side of a block, but by a corridor through the living rooms and across the *pastas* in those on the north side. Many houses had upper floors, with bedrooms over the living rooms and open balconies over the porticoes.

Fittings and finds helped identify the use of some rooms. The best room in the house is usually the men's dining room (*andron*). It is often recognizable from a low cement platform set around the walls as a dais for the dining couches, the pebble mosaic or plastered floor in the center, the painted walls, and the

Crested helmets. *Above:* Argos helmet with
horsehair crest restored; an archaic helmet
with ram's-head crest and silver mane;
crested Corinthian helmet from the "statue
of Leonidas", Sparta; crested Attic helmet
from an Athenian vase by Exekias (*ca.* 530 B.C.).
*Below:* Statuettes with crested Attic and Corinthian
helmets; Thracian helmet, survival, and a crested parallel worn by
Achilles on a cup by the Penthesilea Painter (*ca.* 455 B.C.); Corinthian
helmet with horn-like crest holders.

door set off center, to left or right according to the number of
couches accommodated. Stone funeral couches in tombs elsewhere (such as at Calydon on the north side of the gulf of
Corinth) and banquet scenes on vases help us restore the pattern. The men reclined on their left sides upon couches of single-
bed size (6 by 3 Greek feet, or about 1·80 by ·09 meters) and
ate their food off individual "coffee tables" set alongside each
couch. The couches were set end to end along the walls, overlapping at the corners in such a way that the foot of a couch, never
its head, was set into the corner of the room so as to give a free-
head position to each man. There are ancient references to
dining rooms with three, four, five, seven, and nine couches (and

*Dining rooms*

ΕΡΛΟΝΑΡΙΣΤΟΚΛΕΟΣ

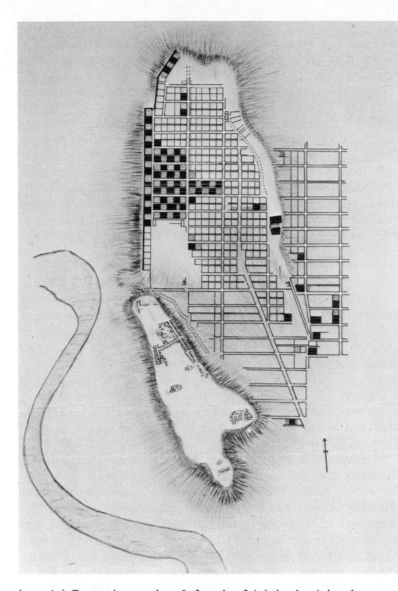

(*opposite*) Composite corselets. *Left:* stele of Aristion by Aristocles (*ca.* 500 B.C.) with Corinthian helmet restored. *Right:* examples from red-figured vases. *Above:* two figures fastening corselet at front, Achilles in a side-fastened corselet with reinforced front; youth receives panoply of helmet, scaled cuirass (back view) and greaves. *Below:* Achilles and Patroclus in scaled corselets.

63

bigger ones in public buildings), and we can restore the pattern of several Olynthian *androns* from their size and the position of the doorway which depends on the set of couches on that side of the room.

Other recognizable rooms are the living room which sometimes has a central hearth, the cooking kitchen with flagged floor, the bathroom with embedded terra-cotta hip bath and plastered floor, the storeroom with its embedded *pithoi,* or great storage jars, and the workroom or loom room where the women wove their homemade clothes and coverlets. The last is sometimes identifiable from the large number of loom weights found inside, used to keep taut the free-hanging warp of the then standard vertical loom.

*Food*     Of the food cooked and eaten in a Greek household we have, not surprisingly, few well-preserved samples. It was a freak of nature that preserved at Pompeii, under the lava of Vesuvius, meals set ready on tables but never eaten, so we can look today at the forms of carbonized loaves, dishes of eggs, and bowls of walnuts. But in Greece we are not without some archaeological evidence. At several places have been found the remnants of many a meal—scattered olive stones and meat bones. At Olynthus itself, pork, goat, beef, venison, and mutton bones were found in the ash of a cooking hearth and the raw material of other meals in storage jars—the charred remains of olives and wheat. Far older were the olives found in 1964, perfectly preserved within a small pot in the Minoan palace at Kato Zakro in eastern Crete.

Epigraphy has given us some lists of household food stocks. Examples are seen on the fragments so far found in Athens of the Attic Stelai. These were eleven or more marble slabs, originally about 1 meter wide and 1·5 meters high, covered with inventories of the confiscated and auctioned property of men condemned for sacrilege in 415 B.C., for parodying the Eleusinian mysteries (the ancient equivalent of celebrating a black mass). The lists contain not only farms, houses, workshops, slaves, furniture, soft furnishing, and clothes, but also the contents of kitchen and stores, such as wheat, millet, barley, lentils, herbs, figs, almonds, grapes, olives, oil, wine, and vinegar. The archaeological material can be filled out with a great mass of literary evidence, ranging from the facetious descriptions of

64     banquets, with lists of tasty dishes, by the comic poets of the

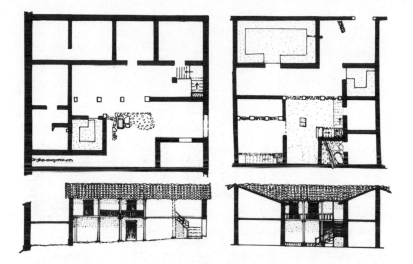

Olynthian houses: plan of a house built up against the city wall and of
a typical house in an ordinary block of ten. Reconstruction sketches
(viewed as from within the courts).

fifth and fourth centuries B.C., to philosophical works on diets
and the properties of edible plants. It is mainly the richness of
these sources that illuminates this aspect of Greek life.

Of the means of storing, cooking, and serving the food and
drink, we have plentiful remains; the containers were, after all,
more durable than the contents. There have survived some
remarkable examples of silver cups and bowls and large bronze
ewers, which show that the rich in classical times sometimes ate
off silver plate and appreciated well-furnished tables. However,
clay was the commonest material for all uses. Pottery of every
sort has been found, in every kind of condition: hundreds of
complete vessels, toilet- and table-ware deposited in graves;
sealed wine jars dredged up from the seabed from ancient
wrecks; waterpots from the bottom of cisterns and wells; and
thousands of pots, chipped, cracked, or—mostly—smashed to
smithereens. The variety of form and size, of fabric and surface,
is in itself revealing. The painted, molded and glazed bowls and
cups, plates and jugs, are likely to have served at table, the red

*Table and
kitchen
furnishings*

65

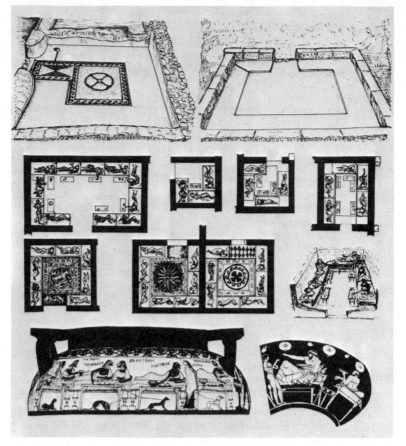

Dining rooms. *Above:* two sketches of excavated dining rooms with low platform for dining couches, one at Olynthus and one at Haleis in the Argolid. *Center:* plans of the dining rooms of some Olynthian houses showing the arrangement of couches and diners, with a thumb-nail reconstruction sketch. *Below:* dining scenes from vases; left, from an early-Corinthian column-*krater* of the late seventh century B.C., and right, from an Attic red-figured cup of the late fifth century B.C.

and buff unglazed crocks in the kitchen, the thin gritty fireproof vessels for cooking, the grids of similar fabric for grilling. Grooved blocks of lava suggests hand querns for grinding; bronze and terra-cotta stands suggest braziers for charcoal broiling. Confirmation is provided by models and by pictures on some of the pots themselves. Terra-cotta statuette groups act out miniature cookery demonstrations: doll-like cooks grind corn, mix meal, and bend over oven, grill, or cooking pot—tiny replicas of life-size objects found in the ruins of houses. And on many of the painted vases the mute objects discovered by excavation are depicted in use in scenes of daily life, and so explained. For instance, on a large open bowl a banquet scene shows an identical vessel in use as a punch bowl from which the wine is ladled into cups and goblets, and another vessel of odd shape may be shown standing in an open bowl, clearly used as a wine cooler. Finally, literary evidence—descriptions of symposia or drinking feasts or cooks in comedies waxing eloquent about their pots and pans—helps us identify the various shapes, not all with certainty. So we learn to call the punch bowl a *krater*; the cups and goblets *skyphoi, kylikes,* and *kantharoi*; the pitcher a *chous*; the wine jug an *oinochoe*; the lidded bowl a *lekanis*; an open one a *lekane*; cooking pots *chytriai*; low casseroles *lopades*; and water jars *hydriai*.

Finally, we turn from the food that Greeks ate to consider how they obtained it. The livelihood of most Greeks was linked with the land. Work on farms would be combined not only with village but also with city life, for farmers (unlike their counterparts in northern Europe) tended to live together in communities and walked or rode out daily to the fields outside the town—a custom still followed today in much of Italy and Greece. Most states were ultimately based on a peasant economy. However, since the land could in many states produce a surplus crop it could also maintain a leisured or ruling class free of the need to work all the time or even at all, and also groups of specialized craftsmen producing tools and necessaries for the peasantry, luxury articles for the rich, and works of art for individuals or the state. All this would promote a trading economy. The Spartans, we have been told, owned two-fifths of the Peloponnesus, and as they had a large serf population called helots to farm the land, the full citizens were free to train as full-time soldiers (provided each could keep up the due contribution to the common mess funds from his own estate), but to prevent strain or competition, industry and commerce were cut back to a minimum. Elsewhere citizens were soldiers only at need and were freer to develop various enterprises. In Attica overproduction of oil and wine led to an export trade in those products, stimulated the container industry of the potter, and allowed the Athenians to import corn of which they could not produce enough. Other places like Chios, Thasos, Rhodes, and Knidos also produced wine for export, and that too meant for them the production of vast numbers of the common two-handled wine jars called amphorae.

Closely datable archaeological evidence of farming is hard to find, for most of the land used in antiquity is still in use today,

Calyx krater

Pelike

Kylikes

Skyphoi

Pottery shapes. Various types of Attic painted and black-glazed forms of the sixth to fourth centuries B.C.

67

*Farming* and digging and ditching and replanting have meant constant disturbance. Further, much of the farmer's regular work was of the kind that would leave no permanent trace; his tools would be removed from the fields (except for broken ones abandoned and perhaps found accidentally by modern farmers) while his crops and trees would have perished, even allowing for the long life of the olive tree. But he might have left his mark on the landscape at large—in the form of irrigation channels and field boundaries still traceable. The archaeologist can then profitably follow up some clues. He may study land utilization by trying to recognize in a landscape fields, terraces and homesteads of earlier times. He may survey and excavate farmhouses and farm buildings. And he may consider the hardware and plant of farm work—tools, mills, winepresses, cisterns, vats, and so on, items which he may well find in towns as well as on isolated farms.

In many parts of Greece it is possible to see abandoned field systems, the clearest to the eye often being hillsides terraced for cultivation but no longer worked. On the coast of Attica, south of Athens, and on the flanks of Hymettus, in an area that had been pasture since the 1880's and had been more recently plowed as large open fields (and is now being rapidly swallowed up in suburb and villa development), a pattern of earlier field terraces was recognized from wartime air photographs. Some were still clear, others plowed over but marked as low banks. It is difficult to date such development (unlike the characteristic Roman pattern of grid division of land called centuriation, which has been noted, again from air photographs, in Italy and Yugoslavia and which can often be closely linked with the known and datable foundation of *coloniae,* or "settlements," of demobilized soldiers). But since as many as five demes existed in that area, it is quite possible that the terracing represented intense land utilization by a heavy population in classical times.

Elsewhere, at some Greek colonial sites, remarkable examples of rectangular field-systems have been identified, notably at Metapontum in southern Italy and as far north as the Crimea. There, on the Heraclean peninsula Russian archaeologists have plotted a whole series of farms occupied by the colonists of ancient Chersonesos. They were able to recognize rectangular plots used as vineyards (with parallel walls used to retain the thin earth and rock-cut pits sunk to accommodate the vine roots), others used as orchards and fields and farmhouses with towers.

68

When we turn to the nucleus of a farm, we get onto safer
ground. Remains of farmhouses in isolated country are more
likely to be traceable than houses in an ancient city unless the
latter became early a ghost town, decayed and covered only by
its debris and not buried under structures erected by later generations. It is a fair assumption that any ancient country dwell-
ing was a farmhouse, and the size and layout of the buildings
will be of interest. The house itself will no doubt (as at Vari) tell
us something of the farmer's domestic life, but for light on his
work we must look to the farmyard—to enclosures, outbuildings, and fixed plant. The foundations of a building may tell us
very little about the use to which it was put—whether to shelter
animals or store foodstuffs. The lack of solid outbuildings and
enclosures could mean only that sheep and goats may not have
had permanent shelter or were penned in brushwood folds (*man-
drakia*), such as may be seen today on hillsides and near small
farms. But round, leveled areas may be readily identifiable as
threshing floors, very similar to ones still in use, and will show
that corn was one of the local crops. Interesting hints of this
kind have been noted at homesteads in the Sounion area of
Attica and on the island of Siphnos.

At such country sites often the best indication of the crops
raised are the remains of the equipment used in processing
them—such plants as olive crushers, olive presses, wine presses,
vats, and mills. Let us select the one example of olives and olive-
oil. At Olynthus were found parts of olive crushers. One was a
large disk of lavastone, some 0·80 meter in diameter; in use, it
had been rolled on its edge inside a circular trough, being moved
by a long lever arm set on a central axis, and the olives poured
into the trough were crushed into a pulp. The next stage was to
extract the oil by dousing the pulp in hot water, enclosing it in a
great bag or in several folds of cloth or grass matting, and to
place the mass on a press bed, having runnels to guide the
extract into a container, and squeezing it under a press beam,
using the leverage of a long arm and heavy weights to apply the
pressure. Olynthus produced one or two stone press beds. At
Praisos in Crete British excavators in 1901 found in the corner
of a room in a Hellenistic house a press bed moved just out of
position from under two holes in the stone wall; these they
thought to be the sockets for a press beam forced down by
weights onto a great pile of folded envelopes containing pulp. A

Olives and olive-oil: presses and pots. *Left, above:* corner of a house at Praisos, Crete, showing oil press in position and holes in rear wall for press beam, with sectional view, and sketch of a "separator" pot; below, an Olynthian oliver crusher, and a cup showing a press in use. *Right:* a black-figured vase showing a scene of olive harvesting.

large pot in the house may have been an oil separator, for it had a spout at the bottom from which the water in the extract could be drained off when the lighter oil rose to the surface of the mixture. Art supplies illustrations of the process, and we may note two as showing aspects of the olive-oil industry. One shows an olive press in use, the lever, the great weights, the pile of pulp containers, and two men operating the machine, one hanging onto the press beam while the other attaches the weights. The other pot illustrates a much earlier stage—a delightful scene of harvesting, with one man in a tree shaking branches and the other on the ground beating the branches with long sticks to make the olives fall—a scene common enough today in Greece.

*Spinning*      Greek farmers also kept sheep and goats for milk, meat, and wool. It was the women's work to spin and weave homemade clothes. Hard evidence of this is to be found in two classes of commonplace objects, found often in great numbers but not very useful for close dating. The first is the spindle whorl, a stone or clay disk or cone, perhaps glazed, pierced for the insertion of

70      the spindle—a short stick around which the thread was to wind

itself; the spindle was given a twirl and allowed to drop slowly from the hand at the end of a thread, which was paid out and spun in the process, from a mass of wool held under the arm. The process is one still to be seen in many villages in Greece. The other class of objects is the loom weight, conical or pyramidical in shape, usually of clay and often glazed. By the ring fixed in the hole at its narrower end, one such loom weight would keep several threads in the vertical warp straight and taut while the weft was woven from side to side and then pushed upward to tighten the fabric. Large numbers found together may hint at the size of loom used, but more useful are vase paintings of such looms in use.

Cloth made in this way was often home-dyed with organic dye made from plants and seaweed. But it might be sent to a village or local dyeworks set up to cater for a cottage industry or even a larger export trade. Ancient Corinth was famous in antiquity for its cloth industry, and at nearby Rachi, on a hill overlooking the Isthmus of Corinth, American excavators found evidence of a stage in its production, a dye works of the fourth century B.C. The hilltop had many cisterns and channels to meet the heavy demand on water. There were four establishments, each consisting of tanks of various sizes cut into the rock. Some were lined with cement to hold liquid, one of these being large and rectangular, with two smaller circular vats at one end of it. Modern analogies from Palestine helped confirm the identification as dye works and to explain the process of successive submersion of clothes inside the round vats. Loom weights found scattered in great numbers suggested that weaving was part of the same industry. Votive pots and a Doric column capital on the hilltop hinted at a shrine there perhaps embodying the communal feeling of the weavers and dyers of this locality (rather like a guild chapel) ; a recent suggestion is that the cult was that of *Athena Phoinike* ("the Purple") mentioned in literary records and interpreted now as a direct link with the purple or dye industry of Corinth.

From vats and cisterns connected with dyeing, we move to rather similar installations used in silver and lead mining in Attica in the area of Laurion. The mines were active between the fifth and late second centuries B.C. They belonged to the state but were generally worked by leascholders, contractors using slave labor. The mines were reopened in 1860 by a French company

## Mining

and the French School of Archaeology cooperated with them in a study of the ancient workings. The investigators found and planned several of the narrow squared tunnels, only a meter or so high, along which the slaves had crawled to the faces, picking away in the light of oil lamps and dragging the ore back in bags to the shafts. Once on the surface, the ore was crushed and then washed to separate the heavier lead particles from the lighter dross of earth and stone. This was done at several *ergasteria,* or "work sites," set often in dells to which surface water was led by channels into cisterns. The washery consisted of a rock-cut or built-up tank, an inclined "table" in front of it and a flatter one beyond, with a channel around its four sides, having deeper catchment basins at the corners. Water seeped continuously from holes at the bottom of the tank, washed over the crude ore on the inclined face, carrying it into the channel and along its whole length, allowing the heavier particles to settle in the first corner basins and sweeping the dross onto the last. The water could be baled back into the tank, the contents of the basins piled in heaps on the flat table to dry, and the process of refining repeated. Eventually the good ore was sent to the furnaces where lead and silver would be extracted.

Ancient workings were found in the hills as far north as Thorikos and beyond. And at Thorikos, on the coast, a Belgian expedition has recently spent some seasons excavating part of the ancient town, uncovering an industrial quarter where several such washing tables were found, with the surfaces and channels well cemented and in extremely good preservation.

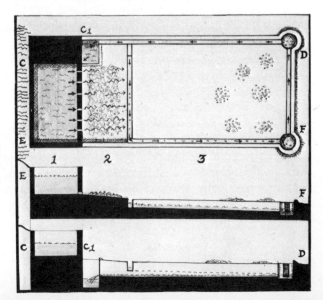

A typical ore-washing table in the silver-mining area of Laurion, plan and section.

72

Epigraphy contributes to our knowledge of this industry, for the American excavations in the Athenian Agora have brought to light a great many fragments of inscribed stone recording the terms of state leases or mining concessions, naming the parties concerned, and defining the area of operation by references to local landmarks.

There is a class of inscriptions found on the Athenian Acropolis known as the Catalog of Silver Saucers which we shall mention as a last example of archaeological evidence for the range of trades found in that city and its environs. These record, in small and abbreviated script on once large but now very fragmentary marble slabs, the dedications to Athena of silver dishes of a standard weight by the winning party in breach of contract cases between freedmen and their ex-masters. These record either the ex-slave's acquittal, his release from a client relationship, and his recognition as a free agent of metic, that is, "resident alien," status, or the patron's victory and the freedman's return to slave status. So the formulas correspond to either "Polytimus, saddler resident in Collytus, released from Kallias, son of Kalliades of Paiania, a salver of 100 drachmas' weight," or "Lysiades, son of Chion of Alopeke, on regaining Sostrate, weaver resident in Melite, a salver of 100 drachmas' weight." The purpose was to register persons of disputed states as freedmen or slaves. The interest for us is that, whereas citizens are listed in the usual way—by name, father's name (patronymic), and hereditary deme, or parish—the inscriptions identify freedmen and aliens by name, trade, and parish of residence, and so suggest to us both the variety of trades and their locations. We can list goldsmiths, blacksmiths or tinkers, signet-ring makers, tanners, saddlers, shoemakers, cobblers, upholsterers, wool workers, farmhands, vine dressers, traders, stall holders, ironmongers, bakers, fishmongers, greengrocers, hemp sellers, cooks, musicians, muleteers, donkeymen, porters, carriers, laborers, valets, nurses, housemaids, scribes, and horse dealers.

These few examples, which could have been extended to so many aspects of life, public as well as private, will suffice to show how much is known about the social history of the classical Greeks, and that archaeology, combining profitably with other sources, has very greatly contributed to the illumination of a past world.

# CHAPTER FOUR

# Studies and Problems

In considering the light thrown on the past by archaeology, we have spotlighted only a few aspects of private life. This was certainly not because of a lack of material. For the classical period, our information is very rich and varied. Volumes could be written on private and public antiquities by combining archaeological with literary evidence. Not that we know all that we would like to about the classical Greeks; much is still dark and there are many problems unsolved. But it is fair to note that (mainly because so much of Greek literature has survived from as early as the sixth and fifth centuries B.C., and hundreds of written records besides) we already know far more about these Greeks than we shall ever discover about some other peoples.

In some countries archaeologists have to deal with the cultures of quite anonymous people whom they have to identify for lack of a better term by a typical artifact or an important archaeological site, and so they have had to talk of "Urnfield people" or "Beaker folk" or "Villanovans." Think of it! It is as if we knew the fifth century B.C. Athenians no more intimately than as the "Red-figured pot people!" This would indeed be the case if we had not a scrap of the writings of Aeschylus, Sophocles, Euripides, Herodotus, Thucydides, Xenophon, Lysias, and Aristophanes, and had never heard of Miltiades, Themistocles, Pericles, and Socrates. In some areas, for long ages of prehistory, we cannot name a single individual. But more than thirty thousand ancient Athenians are known to us by name, and many of the famous or infamous by character and reputation. In comparison with the yawning gaps, never to be bridged, in our knowledge of some other peoples, the blanks in our coverage of the classical Greeks seem only hairline cracks.

One effect of this happy state of affairs has been the development of the various special branches of study referred to in the first chapter—the result of there being such a mass of evidence

74

to be worked on. Apart from excavations in the field, a great deal of work has been done over the years to codify and clarify and interpret the material. Another effect is that classical archaeologists have more and more devoted their exploratory efforts—field surveys and excavation—to the earliest periods of Greek archaeology, to the prehistory pioneered by Schliemann, Dörpfeld, Tsountas, and Arthur Evans, who revealed civilizations hardly known at all from written records, purely by their efforts with the spade. It is in these earliest periods that the gaps are widest, and here that excavation might revolutionize our knowledge. Here, too, actual digging is followed by great efforts to compare and classify the finds and to collect and decode the scantier written records in the linear scripts.

In this chapter we will describe this background of solid achievement in the past, and in dealing with the problems of the present and future, we will have to mention some that appear questions of detail; the answers, even if they turn out to be unexpected, may not upset the general picture of the classical period. Even so, classical archaeologists have no cause to rest on their spades. We may already know much about Athens and some other famous states, but there is more to learn; and about other cities and communities which have left us little literature, we have a great deal still to seek out.

Athens has for centuries been studied. In the 1620's the Dutchman Meursius collected ancient literary references to its antiquities; the Capuchin monks prepared a map; the antiquarians pried about in the corners of the old town; Morosini's engineers prepared plans and drawings of the city and Acropolis (which hardly made up for his gunners' blowing up of the Parthenon in 1687) ; Stuart and Revett spent 3 years measuring and sketching; and archaeologists of many nations have excavated and studied at great cost in money, effort, and time. The topographers of the past have found the sites of most of the famous cities of antiquity, and have discovered, noted, and studied the great majority of the standing ruins. However, there are many ancient cities, towns, and villages, unnamed even in the surviving literature, that still await a thorough survey and the kind of exploration that stops short of excavation. Some may well have not been very important in Panhellenic politics, and yet if they were carefully surveyed, and particularly if some were excavated, they would throw a flood of light on life in their 75 particular region. Arcadia and northwestern Greece have much to reveal. In recent years several towns and cities have been identified in Epirus and southern Albania, many of which were doubtless among the seventy cities destroyed by the Roman general L. Aemilius Paulus in his punitive campaign against the ancient Epirotes in 167 B.C.

There are several places known from ancient literature to have existed, indeed to have been important, which have not yet been exactly located. Sometimes the difficulty is one of choosing between two or more possible sites, and then the solution may have to await the test of excavation. That was the case at Troy until Schliemann's excavations of 1870, and again at Olynthus until Professor Robinson's excavations of 1928. In other cases the name remains while the site itself seems to have vanished. A particular and unusual case is that of Helice, a city of Achaea on the southern shore of the Gulf of Corinth. We are told by Pausanias, Strabo, and Aelian that it was very suddenly submerged by the sea in one single night in 373 B.C. Since then, the land surface might have risen again so part of the ancient city may be free of the waters once more but buried deep beneath the silt of the former seabed. Professor Marinatos, head of the Greek Archaeological Service, has drawn attention in recent years to the great possibilities of the site as a Greek Pompeii, cut off in its classical prime, petrified under a capping of alluvial soil rather than ash and lava; he has examined the region where Helice was traditionally located, identified its probable site and invited international cooperation in its exploration. Already various American university teams have tested the coastal waters with electronic equipment to try to trace by echo devices the solider remains of the city below the gravel and silt of the seabed, and further attempts, including perhaps drilling, are to follow.

*Underwater*
*researches*

The underwater mapping of less deeply submerged remains has been carried out with success at Haleis, on the Argolid coast, on the east side of the Peloponnesus. An American team from Indiana University and the University of Pennsylvania has conducted some excavations on land and planned the flooded parts of the city walls and harbor by combining the close work of underwater divers, measuring and drawing stone by stone, with the bird's-eye view of an overhead camera suspended high in the air above the remains, attached to a captive balloon. The

76

balloon could be moved along to the required spot by its guide rope, anchored or held in place by a diver, and the camera triggered off by remote control; and then the whole operation repeated further along the line of the submerged walls. With special film the objects under the water would show up clearly and a series of prints could be made, overlapping so as to give a photographic map of everything preserved in place. From these and the probing of the divers, an accurate plan of the submerged walls and towers was prepared; and so a new technique of field-work was perfected.

Air photography has not played quite such an outstanding part in Greek topographical studies as it has in Britain, where it has transformed the map of Roman Britain, adding scores of Roman forts and villas and native settlements, and has also thrown new light on earlier and later periods on the island. Seen from the air, buried or plowed-out sites have been recognized either from crop marks—the differences in growth and color observed in growing or in ripening crops or variations in parched meadows, caused by the presence of stone structures or deeper soil-filled ditches under the surface—or else from shadows cast by very slight undulations when picked out by oblique light or thin drifts of snow. Yet in Greece it has been used with profit in some areas, and its use as an illustration of former field patterns has been already noted. A particular achievement has been the recovery of the "Hippodamian" plan of ancient Rhodes. Air photographs picked out the regularity of some of the streets of the medieval and modern city (which overlies a small part of the ancient one) and the extension of some of these lines beyond into the open country, where the field boundaries follow the same alignments. This evidence was confirmed by finding streets and buildings in small rescue excavations over the years, and it has been possible to restore almost the whole ancient street plan in outline. *Air photography*

Modern studies in architecture take note of all the buildings of an ancient settlement because all, the meanest as well as the monumental, can tell us something about the inhabitants. The monumental remains of antiquity naturally enough took the attention of early antiquarians; these were the most imposing ruins to be seen above ground and they represented the supreme effort and ideal of ancient Greek architects. Surviving temples were measured, drawn, and reconstructed by generations of *Architecture* architects and artists—they saw in them the noblest work of their ancient masters, and some they copied in their own buildings.

Temples The Greek temple is basically a simple form of building, which can be derived from the great halls of Mycenaean kings and Homeric heroes. The essential is a rectangular shrine, or cella, with a gable roof, and a door at one end, fronted usually by columns set clear of the front wall or between extensions of the side walls (*in antis*) ; embellishments added to the type were a rear porch, false or opening into a rear chamber (*opisthodomos*), and a freestanding series of columns set all around the shrine (*peripteron*), standing on the edge of the enlarged platform base and supporting the eaves and gable-end pediments of an enlarged, projecting roof. There are some temples of revolutionary design, but even those belonging to the established type show several variations, some quite subtle; the search for perfection in proportions led to constant refinements of detail.

Parthenon One of the best studied of Greek temples is without doubt the Parthenon, the temple of Athena Parthenos ("the Maiden"). Cyriaco of Ancona was one of the first "modern" students of the building, and he made sketches of which copies still exist, though these are rather odd with some elements very out of place. Practically all the early visitors to Athens noted and described the temple—the cathedral church as it was for centuries until it became a mosque sometime after the Turkish capture of the Acropolis in 1458. The Marquis de Nointel's unknown artists made twenty-one drawings of the building and its sculptures in 1674, including both pediments, thirty-two of the metope panels above the peripteral columns and much of the frieze along the top of the cella wall. Though not done in exact detail, as the artists were not allowed to use scaffolding to enable them to draw at close quarters, these sketches are of great archaeological value now because thirteen years later an explosion destroyed so much of the building. Draftsmen of the eighteenth century who contributed to the study and publication of the Parthenon included Dalton (1749), Stuart and Revett (1751–53), and, later, William Pars, who climbed up onto the architrave or lintel beams of the columns to get a close-up view. In the nineteenth century scholars by the score studied this building. Among the notable ones were Bronstedt, a Dane, Allison and Cockerell who noted the *entasis,* or the swelling, of the columns toward their middle, John Pennethorpe (1837), Hoffer and Schaubert (1838), and F. C. Penrose (1846–47), all of whom studied the curvatures of the lines of the building and its subtle optical refinements; the Frenchman Paccard (1845) and the Englishman Knowles who drew accurate new plans, and the American E. P. Andrews who in 1896 deciphered a Roman inscription of 61 A.D. on the architrave from the holes left by nails holding the bronze letters to the marble. This century has seen studies, which have included several new minor discoveries about the sculptural arrangements, by Rhys Carpenter, Charles Picard, G. P. Stevens, and most recently by Frank Brommer who made new casts of all the sculptures still in place and the sockets of statues now elsewhere so as to study the groupings and subjects anew. The epigraphers have added their quota of knowledge. As fragments of the building inscriptions of the Parthenon and of some other Acropolis buildings have survived, much can be learned about the plans of the architects, the contracts, the expenses of materials and labor, the organization of gang work, and the stages of erection. These show that the Parthenon was started in 447–446 B.C., erected by 438, and embellished with all its statuary by 432 B.C. So, continuous study over the years has made this masterpiece one of the best-known Greek temples.

The problems involved in studying temples depends partly on whether or not a particular example is well preserved and partly on how closely it followed the regular type in plan and in the rules of the Doric, Ionic, or Corinthian orders. Two extremes of preservation are represented at Athens, in temples sited very close together. One is the temple of Hephaestus, the so-called *Theseum,* probably the best-preserved temple in all Greece because it was turned into a church, and so kept in fair repair, while, unlike the Parthenon, it was not on a lofty hill likely to be defended—and bombarded. From the outside it looks as if very little had changed since it was erected, on the low Colonus hill on the west edge of the Agora, about 449–444 B.C. To restore its original appearance, even that of its interior, is not so very difficult. Very different was the case of its nearest neighbor, the temple of Ares, god of war, a little beyond the foot of the hill, in the Agora itself. This was discovered only in the course of the American excavations and then only as a leveled foundation

*Temple of Hephaestus*

*Temple of Ares*

79

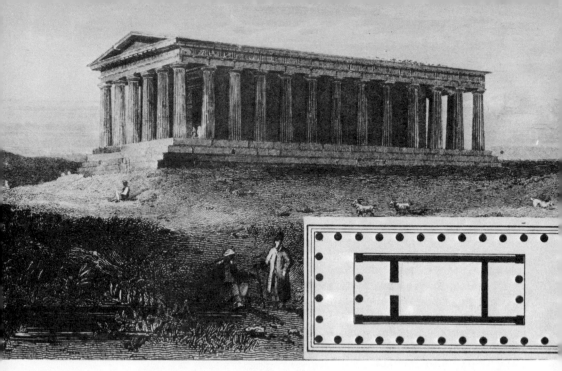

The "Theseum": survival of perfected form, an early nineteenth-century view of the best-preserved temple in Greece (from H. W. Williams, *Views in Greece*, 1829), with an inset plan.

with some scattered blocks of the upper structure. W. B. Dinsmoor, the American scholar, saw that not only had it suffered almost total destruction, but sometime in antiquity it had been bodily removed from its first site to its present one in the Agora. From its cornice blocks, almost identical with those of the Hephaestus temple, he concluded that it was in size and style very similar to that temple, with six Doric columns along the front and thirteen along the sides, perhaps a later work of the same architect. That it had been resited in Roman times was noted both from the form of the foundation—a platform of the type then favored—and from the early imperial-period lettering cut on each block to help the dismantling and the rebuilding of the temple stone by stone.

A somewhat different problem faced Dinsmoor when he studied the largest temple in the Peloponnesus, not from its foundations and its site—which were in fact not known to him—but from a single fragment of column and a mutilated block of the superstructure, both reused in a Venetian fortification at

Temple oddities. The Erechtheum at Athens; above: reconstruction of east end (after G. P. Stevens) with north porch to right; below, plan showing roofed area dotted (and site of sacred olive tree in temple yard outside), with the south (caryatid) porch to left.

Corinth. The size and fluting enabled him to restore a Doric column, which, if built in the right proportion of height to thickness, would be more than 2 meters in diameter and more than 11 meters high, and such could only have been intended for an unusually large temple. The proportions of the architrave block allowed him to calculate that the vanished temple had measured about 29 by 73 meters, or some 40 by 90 meters on its stylobate, or platform top, depending on whether it had six or eight columns along its front. Further, he conjectured that these details dated the temple to the fifth century B.C.

Not all temples were conventional in plan or confined to the normal features of the three Greek orders. The Erechtheum on the Athenian Acropolis is one well-preserved example of a very odd temple, built with side porches, one having caryatids, or marble maidens, to support its roof, and with different floor levels and Ionic columns of different height, so as to enclose several already established cults in one shrine. Another example of an odd building, but one with nothing left standing on its 81 platform base, was the huge temple of Olympian Zeus at the Greek colony of Akragas (now Agrigento) in Sicily. Studied and restored by C. R. Cockerell in 1812 and again by the German Robert Koldewey in 1894, it has been redrawn as having an ordinary enough rectangular plan but one with its outer Doric columns linked with walls and with stone giants set between the columns, as if for extra support.

With less formal types of buildings, less tied to the norms of the classical orders, complete excavation is the best basis for studying and restoring them.

*Ceramics*  Excavation has likewise provided the material for the study of Greek vases and also helped date particular varieties to their period of manufacture and use. The historical study of pottery development has grown up internally too, through the ever more detailed classification of vases by type and style, the examination of techniques of pot manufacture and decoration, and the identification of regional schools of painting and of individual artists and their disciples. Painted pottery has received more attention because it has been collected and admired so long for its artistic merit, and because it is more distinctive, offers better clues when fragmentary, and exhibits quicker changes of fashion and style than most coarse pots.

*Painted vases*  Sir William Hamilton in the eighteenth century was among the pioneers of Greek vase studies when he published the lovely examples that he had collected. Since then, a vast number of books and articles have appeared, some putting on record small groups of whole pots recovered from tombs, or potsherds showing some interesting local or period variety, others being catalogs of vast museum collections, often of pots which have to be studied without an exact archaeological context since their findspot was not known. The following few examples will suggest some period classifications and special aspects of vase painting. For the earlier Dark Age and Archaic periods we have V. R. d'A. Desborough's *Protogeometric Pottery* and J. N. Coldstream's *Greek Geometric Pottery*. General surveys and fine illustrations of the whole field are provided in R. M. Cook's *Greek Painted Pottery* and Arias, Hirmer, and Shefton's *History of Greek Vase Painting*. Richter's *Shapes and Names of Athenian Vases* classified the types and tried to fit accurately ancient names to the known varieties of surviving pots, while J. V. 82 Noble's *Techniques of Painted Attic Pottery* analyzed the whole complex process, the very chemistry, of producing the deep rich black glaze which was typical of classical vases. Students of vase painting have recently lost their master in this field, Sir John Beazley. A distinguished pupil declared that his individual efforts (in such comprehensive works as *The Development of Attic Black-Figure, Attic Black-Figure Vase-Painters,* and *Attic Red-Figure Vase-Painters*) made the study of classical Athenian pottery a field of art history in which his successors would be able to recognize at once all the chief painters and many of the minor ones; he concluded that the main work in this sector had been done. But there would still be room for further effort, to try to distinguish even further between the earlier and later work of known master painters.

The less artistic classes of pottery, the undecorated glazed, or semiglazed and coarse wares, have received increasing attention in the last 30 to 40 years. One motive has been the need to be able to date as closely as possible sites which have produced little or no artistic wares. Another has been the urge to study trade contacts, through such things as imported wine jars and the official city seals or stamps upon some of them (corresponding to the châteaux labels of good modern vintages), and yet another has been to illustrate some aspects of everyday life with these household possessions. The publication of a corpus of some particular class of pot found in great numbers on some large site has often been a great step forward. Thus the volumes on the Olynthus pottery illustrated the whole range of coarse and fine pottery over about a century of time. The volumes on the Athenian Agora, published or in preparation, cover whole classes such as Greek lamps, Roman lamps, coarse classical pottery, and Hellenistic pottery.

The dating of Hellenistic coarse pottery has not been worked out as accurately as that of the classical. However, the excavation of some sites of known historical dates, occupied briefly or in several datable phases, would greatly help give absolute dates to such material. The problems can be illustrated by the case of a site explored 10 years ago, the fortified encampment on the Koroni peninsula on the east coast of Attica. The finds included much material not typical of an Attic site, such as imported wine-jar fragments and Egyptian coins of Ptolemy II (who reigned 285–246 B.C.). History provided a suitable occasion for a foreign coastal base in the activities of an Egyptian fleet sent to

Ancient wine-jars, sixth to fifth centuries B.C.

83

protect Athens and establish strong points during a war against Macedonia in 266–261 B.C. The difficulty was that the Hellenistic pottery, mainly coarse ware, and the amphora stamps resembled types hitherto thought to be 30 to 40 years earlier. Also, some sherds were found together, obviously used and broken at the same time, representing varieties of a class of plate which were thought, in terms of classifying and dating from shape alone, to indicate earlier and much later forms of that dish. Such apparent disagreements may well be found in any class of archaeological material in which the classification is still not closely fixed. More material and the chance to compare groups from accurately dated sites will also help clarify the phases of Hellenistic pottery.

*Epigraphy*     Epigraphy exhibits, as do other branches, some of the achievements and problems of scholars. Inscriptions of every sort have been avidly copied, interpreted, and published ever since Cyriaco collected them in the fifteenth century or William Petty brought to England in 1627 the famous "Parian Marble" which offered classical historians the convenience of a long list of dates and events. Compiled by some Hellenistic antiquarian of Paros, it dated entries as so many years before its final item, the presidency of Diognetus, archon of Athens in 264–263 B.C., and starts with Cecrops, the first king of Athens, said to be 1,318 years earlier (that is, 1581 B.C.!). Since then, epigraphists have collected examples of the whole range of regional alphabets used by the Greeks, borrowed by them from the Phoenicians (as the historian Herodotus concluded from his inquiries in the fifth century B.C.), and they can date them from the letter forms and the layout of the texts. Some early inscriptions were written in an odd way, the lines alternately from left to right and then right to left, with the words spelled out and even the letters written in reverse. This was the *boustrophedon,* or "ox-plow," style, named after the single-bladed plow dragged to and fro across a field, changing direction at the end of each furrow. A notable example is the huge inscription setting out an archaic law code of Gortyn in Crete.

Later conventions include both wording separated by gaps or stops, and continuous texts without such, in which the face of the *stele,* or "slab," was sometimes divided by fine lines into squares (like graph paper) and a letter was fitted into each, giving an overall pattern (*stoichedon*). The thousands of inscrip-

84

The law code of Gortyn: *boustrophedon* script. A great inscription carved on the rear wall of a Roman odeum at Gortyn: the text reads alternatively from left to right, and (with letters reversed) from right to left.

tions found have illustrated high politics, civil and religious administration, private lawsuits, and a great many other aspects of life. As many are found incomplete or with the inscription mutilated or worn, the task of deciphering them and fitting newfound fragments into already familiar parts of the text is often extremely taxing.

A particularly interesting problem, which has kept scholars busy discussing and writing since 1959, arose from the discovery by an American visitor to Troizen, in the Argolid, of a stone slab inscribed with the text of the Themistocles' Decree. This set out the Emergency Security Regulations passed by the Athenian assembly on the proposal of their great general, to meet the threat of Persian invasion in 480 B.C. The gist of its contents was familiar from Herodotus' description of the embarkation of the Athenian men on the city's war fleet and the evacuation of women, children, and old men to Troizen and the islands of Aegina and Salamis; and references to such a decree occur also in later authors. However, the inscription we have cannot possibly date to 480 B.C., for its lettering and layout should date it to the fourth or early third century B.C. The questions which have vexed scholars are: When was the Troizen copy set up; on what occasion; and why? Some have even asked (since this text

85

differs in some details from Herodotus' order of events) if it is an accurate copy of an original decree or only a paraphrase. It could even be a version doctored to suit some purpose of propaganda 150 years or so after the event, some policy relevant to conditions in the fourth century. Some scholars have doubted whether the Troizen inscription is genuine; others have accepted its accuracy.

*Non-Greek inscriptions*    Rather different in scale of difficulty to the fine points raised by the Themistocles' Decree and many other Greek inscriptions are the handful of inscriptions found in Greece, written in a variety of the Greek alphabet but not in the Greek language. For, just as in modern Greece, there are some groups of Albanian speakers and some Vlachs or nomadic shepherds who speak a Romance tongue not unlike Rumanian, so there were in the archaic and even classical times some minority groups in Greece or the Greek-dominated Aegean who spoke languages now quite unknown.

One such inscription which can be read (so far as following the letters goes) but not understood was found on the island of Lemnos and is now on display in the Athens National Museum. Comparisons have often been drawn between this and Etruscan inscriptions in Italy, but it is by no means clear whether there is

Non-Greek inscriptions. *Above:* the famous stele from Lemnos with warrior's head and inscription; part of an inscription from Samothrace. *Below:* a fourth-century B.C. Eteocretan inscription from Praisos.

a close link between the two languages. The island of Samothrace, also in the north Aegean, has produced not only Greek inscriptions but some non-Greek ones also, and attempts have been made to interpret them by comparisons with what is known of Thracian and Illyrian languages. Again in Crete, at Praisos in the east of the island, there were found by the German Halbherr in 1884 and British School excavators in 1901 and 1904 five fragmentary non-Greek inscriptions. Some were written in the Ionic letters of sixth-century type, others in fourth-century lettering; all were in a language sometimes called Etcocretan ("Old Cretan"). Homer's *Odyssey* described Crete as populated by Achaeans, Eteocretans, Cydonians, Dorians, and Pelasgians, and his words suggest a mingling of languages on the island. Strabo, a geographer, mentioned that Praisos belonged to the Eteocretans who were thought to be aborigines, or natives of the island, and late Greek inscriptions mention the independence of this minority group at Praisos which was ended about 140 B.C. The problem of interpretation is not helped by the shortness of the Eteocretan inscriptions and their style of continuous text written as a series of letters without a clear break between words. Various scholars have tried to recognize some words (that is, groups of letters) as Greek borrowings or as forms related to Phrygian and other Aegean languages. Certainty is not possible at present as the total number of inscriptions is so small. Greek inscriptions were also found at Praisos, suggesting that the population was to some extent bilingual, so the texts written in Eteocretan may never have been very numerous. The problems of Eteocretan, Samothracian and "Lemnian" still await final solution—and may never be solved unless a bilingual text is found, the one intelligible version being a translation or key to the other, or unless enough texts are found for scholars to crack the code by comparing them to see how often various groups of letters occur and testing various suggestions as to their meanings.

Some of the problems facing archaeologists will be solved by new equipment and greater ingenuity and by calling in the resources of science. Others will respond to the refinement of long-established scholarly studies, to patient observation, and to inspired insight. Others again must await further discoveries and new comparative material. However, as fast as old problems are solved, new challenges will always appear.

# CHAPTER FIVE

# Masterpieces and Small Finds

In 1967 Professor Marinatos invited the foreign archaeological schools to assist the Greek Archaeological Service in the challenge suddenly presented by a scheme to form a vast irrigation reservoir in the northwest Peloponnesus. A great part of the Peneios Valley in Elis was to be flooded, and the problem was to recover as much information as possible about the whole history of the area before the waters rose. The schools sent teams to comb the areas allocated to them, to find sites by noting sherds, tiles, and building stones on the surface, to dig trial trenches where necessary and so plot on the map all sites, large and small, of every period, and then to conduct rescue excavations at those of particular interest. In 1969 a group of us from the British School of Archaeology set off to dig in the valley. In seeing us off, the ephor of Olympia used words which must have been used many times before by many archaeologists wishing success to their colleagues; *kali evrimata*—"Have good finds!"

One of the delightful things about Greek archaeology is that one may find not only objects that illuminate the past, but also those that are in themselves things of great beauty, creations of superb artistry even if found in mutilated condition. As it happened, our sites in Elis produced nothing of such quality, but beauty is not often absent from archaeological sites in Greece. Excavators in some other countries may find nothing but artifacts of the poorest sort, things no doubt highly significant in history but crude in artistry. Others elsewhere may hope for finds of ponderous magnificence and laborious workmanship, but of little grace. The Greeks, however, produced so much that was beautiful, elegant, and graceful that in their country the excavator may well have the satisfaction of discovering not only what will solve the problems in his mind but will also please his eye and gladden his heart.

88     It was this possibility that inspired most early excavators.

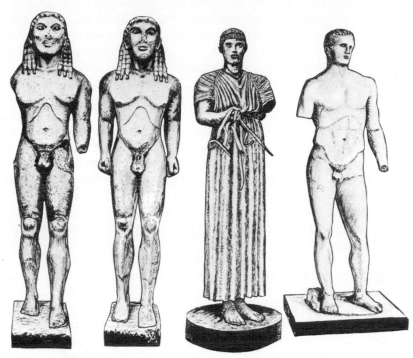

Fine statues from Delphi and
Olympia. Biton and Cleobis (*ca.*
600–590 B.C.); the Delphic
charioteer (*ca.* 475–470 B.C.);
Agias, after Lysippus (325–
300 B.C.). *Below:* Hermes with
infant Dionysos, Olympia.

They were treasure hunters rather than historians researching with the spade, and they usually discarded material that could have been significant but was not artistically pleasing. This attitude was linked with one approach to classical antiquity, that of art history and connoisseurship. The other approach, that of historical research, came later. This regards all material as evidence which can help make the past vivid for us, and it must be the outlook of scientific archaeology. Even so, it will always be an added excitement for the classical archaeologist to recover for the modern world some lost masterpiece of ancient art.

*Statuary from*
*Delphi*
When the French School under Theophile Homolle began their large-scale excavations at Delphi in 1892, it was not long before they unearthed remarkable examples of sculpture. In the second year, when digging along the front of a terrace wall, they discovered a perfect marble statue of a young man with long tresses of hair and that half smile on his face so typical of archaic sculpture. It was an exciting moment, fit to be recorded in a great group photograph which shows the nude *kouros,* knee-deep in a pit, propped up with a post under his chin, gazing with blank eyes at his rescuers, who pose rather awkwardly in their dark suits or shirt sleeves, though one figure stands out, magnificent in the short waistcoat and *fustanella* of national dress. It was certainly a great find and a fine statue; but it was more than just an example of period work to be known thereafter by its findspot or a museum number. For this was Cleobis, one of the very statues mentioned in the first book of Herodotus' *History* in connection with a moral tale said to have been told by Solon of Athens, one of the seven wise men of antiquity, to the millionaire monarch Croesus of Lydia. The very next spring its twin was found, again whole but for its right arm and left hand. Herodotus must have seen these statues, and inscriptions on them assured the finders that these were indeed his Cleobis and Biton. They were the sons of a priestess of Argos, who, when their mother's oxen were not brought in time to draw her cart to a festival at Hera's temple outside Argos, themselves pulled the heavy cart all the way, a distance of 45 *stades,* or 9 kilometers. Their mother prayed that such good sons receive the best gift that Hera could grant, and the goddess caused them to sleep that night in her temple—and to wake no more. The Argives commemorated their dutiful act by commissioning the two statues of the youths and sending them to Del-

phi. Their date must be about 600–590 B.C., judged on their style.

Two years later, in 1896, the French found another magnificent statue, this time a bronze figure of a young charioteer, standing formally erect, still holding parts of the reins in his hand. Again there was a helpful inscription. It named as the dedicator a certain Polyzelos, who was brother of Gelon, tyrant first of Gela and then of Syracuse in Sicily between about 490 and 478 B.C. The group of which this statue formed part must have commemorated a victory in the chariot race at the Pythian games at Delphi. The statue shows some of the severity of the archaic period and the subtleties of the classical. Close study of it has shown that it was made by the lost-wax method (by which a layer of wax between a clay mold and a clay core was melted out to make room for the molten metal). It was cast in seven parts which were then joined together. The youth is dressed in a long tunic with folds almost like the fluting of a column; his hair was engraved not just molded, his headband inlaid with silver and copper, his lips made of copper to deepen their color, and the eyes of white, brown, and black paste.

Another remarkable statue dug up by the French at Delphi was a marble figure of a rather later style. It belonged to a great base which had sockets for nine statues. The one found was identified as Agias, a famous pancratiast (exponent of all-in fighting) and victor three times at Delphi and many times at other Panhellenic games. He and the others were members of a famous family of Pharsalus and ancestors of the dedicator, Daochos, tetrarch of Thessaly in 338–334 B.C. This and more was learned from the verse inscription on the base—and the very same words have been found on a base, devoid of its statues, at Pharsalus itself, and added there was the signature of the famous master sculptor Lysippus. So it has been suggested that the Agias is a marble copy of the bronze originals by the master set up in the dedicator's hometown.

Bases inscribed with the signatures of famous sculptors are, unfortunately, found more commonly than are the superimposed statues. The latter were often looted, sometimes lost during transport, at sea perhaps (and bronzes dragged up in fishermen's nets show that this did happen), or taken off to grace Roman villas and public buildings. Many disappeared forever in bronze foundries or lime kilns. For example, the 91 base of an athlete's statue naming the sculptor as Lysippus and the subject as Poulydamas was found at Olympia, but the statue had gone. Another base signed by the equally famous Praxiteles was found in the Athenian Agora, and again the masterpiece was not found.

*The statue of Hermes at Olympia*

But in 1877 at Olympia the Germans discovered what was claimed as one of the few original creations of a great master. Pausanias visited and described this great religious center in the second century A.D. and mentioned as one of the later works set up in the temple of Hera a marble Hermes bearing the infant Dionysus, a work of Praxiteles. It was in the ruins of this very temple, in one of the bays in its cella, that 1,700 years later the excavators of the German Institute freed from the silt a marble of a young god bearing an infant on his left arm. Here surely was the very work that Pausanias saw and which they believed must be that of the master of the fourth century B.C. Hermes is shown leaning against a wooden post or trunk (a necessary support for marble statues when the center of balance was not directly over the feet), supporting the younger god on his left forearm and raising his right arm, now broken, to hold something out of reach of the infant. The spirit of the work is human, almost playful, rather than remote and awesome, and there is a softness in the treatment of form and surface. The skin is smoothly polished on the front (the back is left less highly finished), the hair is ruffled and was originally colored reddish-brown, the robe over the support rucked and creased, and the sandals gilded. However, the style, the finish, and details of the sculptor's techniques have led some scholars to doubt Pausanias' identification and the fourth century date dependent on it; a date as late as about 100 B.C. has recently been suggested as more probable.

*Phidias*

Olympia had in antiquity possessed one of two colossal gold and ivory (chryselephantine) statues made by the fifth-century master Phidias, a type used only for cult statues inside temples. One was the standing Athena in the Parthenon at Athens, the other the majestic Zeus enthroned in the cella of his temple at Olympia. The technique used was to attach to a wooden core laminated sections of ivory to represent flesh and plates of gold to form robes, helmets, thrones, and the symbols of authority. This combination of materials, precious and perishable, has 92 unfortunately ensured that no example has survived to our day.

Phidias' master-pieces: replica and relics. *Left*: the Varvakeion statuette, a miniature copy of the chryselephantine Athena in the Parthenon. *Center:* bronze coins of Elis depicting the chryselephantine Zeus of Olympia. *Right*: a reconstruction of the Zeus statue. *Below*: Phidias' beaker, with his name on the bottom, and fragments of terracotta molding used for the gold sheeting of the Zeus

Indeed, the gold plates of the Athena statue could be detached, for they served as the city's gold reserves for emergencies. Statuettes modeled on these great works and replicas on coins have given art historians some idea of Phidias' creations. The masterpieces have vanished, but humbler finds made at Olympia in 1955–56 revealed some traces of the master at work. When they 93 excavated the building known as Phidias' workshop (which exactly matched the cella of Zeus' temple in size), the Germans found the tools and materials of the sculptor's trade: a furnace pit and slag from bronze casting, pieces of bronze, iron, lead, plaster, bone and ivory, and, most interesting of all, terra-cotta molds lettered to fit into a known series. On these the gold was beaten so as to form parts of the drapery. And an Attic black-glazed drinking mug, well preserved but not extraordinary in itself, added a human note. Underneath it was neatly scratched the sculptor's name, and probably by his own hand: *Pheidiou* (Phidias' cup).

It must be one of the less thrilling duties of the officers of the Greek Archaeological Service to check on all the holes dug in cities and towns by builders and civil engineers, the road extensions, the house foundations, the pits for oil tanks and the trenches for water pipes and gas mains. Sometimes these expose a corner of an ancient building, the curb of an ancient street, a broken column or a cesspit, the cobbling of a court, or a layer of potsherds. A good deal of useful information has been recorded in this way. Details have been added here and there, like pieces in a jigsaw puzzle, to ancient city plans, and such accidental discoveries have been rewarding, at Rhodes, for instance. Sometimes it has proved worthwhile to open up the workmen's trenches in order to dig more of a building. Often, however, nothing at all has been found, or little really worth recording. What an excitement then it must have been for the Greek archaeologists whose duties have to take in such humdrum tasks to hear that workmen digging sewers in the Piraeus had exposed the hand and arm of a bronze statue. This find made in 1959 proved one of the richest ever and was excavated under the direction of Professor John Papademetriou, who was head of the Archaeological Service at that time. When the area was opened up, there was revealed a hoard of four superb bronze statues, and three marble sculptures, lying on their backs or sides, packed together in a space less than 6 by 6 meters inside what must have been a warehouse. The bronzes included an archaic nude *kouros,* probably an Apollo holding a bow in his left hand. This proved to be the oldest known bronze of its type, dating to about 530–500 B.C. Another statue represented a larger-than-life Athena in peplos and crested helmet decorated with owls and griffins. Formerly she held a shield in her left hand and possibly

*The Piraeus bronzes*

94

a dish, or *phiale,* in her right. There was also a smaller Artemis with a quiver at her back; a Muse or poetess with girdled peplos, and a large bronze tragic mask, perhaps to be linked with the Muse. The female deities were of the middle and late fourth century B.C. Of the marbles one was a half-size female figure, an Eastern goddess or priestess with her arms trussed inside her robe, and the other two were herms, busts of the god Hermes (of a stylized archaic pattern with full beard and long tresses) set upon high pedestals.

It seems that these statues were collected for shipment, possibly to Rome, but the warehouse had been burned down in the first century B.C., perhaps in the siege and sack of the Piraeus in 86 B.C. by the Roman general L. Cornelius Sulla. So the statues had lain forgotten under the cinders and debris for eighteen centuries until a chance find enabled archaeologists to recover the whole group. The statues had to be studied, cleaned, and restored, but they will one day become a principal attraction of the new museum now being built in the Piraeus. In 1966, during our work on the Vari material, two of these bronzes, the magnificent Athena and the Muse, were our daily companions, for they lay close to the table where John and I worked in the old museum at the far humbler finds of our own excavation.

Just as there were master sculptors, so there were master *Paintings* painters. The names of several are known, and something of their general style, not from their works, but rather from the comments of ancient admirers and critics. Only a very few examples of painting have survived on marble, on terra-cotta and on wood, and these are hardly real masterpieces.

From a seventh-century shrine in the Athenian Agora came a painted terra-cotta plaque showing a goddess with her head jutting out in relief, her arms upraised, standing between two snakes; the colors used are flat washes of red, green, yellow, and white.

In a cave at Sikyon on the north coast of the Peloponnesus were found four small painted plaques of wood dating to the late sixth century B.C. The colors used were red, brown, blue, black, and white, used in plain washes. The scenes showed human figures; one was of a religious ceremony with a procession of people carrying offerings, while lettering added the names of worshipers and the deities—the nymphs. They must therefore have received worship in this cave as they did in the grotto above the Vari house.

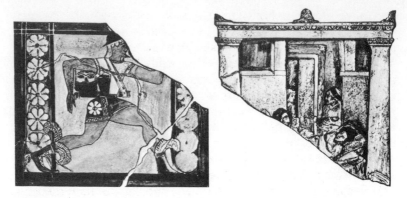

Painting: two survivals. Sketches of a painted metope from the archaic temple at Thermon in Aetolia, showing Perseus carrying Medusa's head (late seventh century B.C.), and of the gravestone of Hediste (third century B.C.).

Larger examples of the same period came from the late sixth-century temple of Apollo at Thermon in Aetolia. Excavation there unearthed the fragmentary terra-cotta metopes which had been set in the gaps between roof timbers, on the outer side of the eaves, above the wooden columns and lintel beams. The plaques are painted in a limited range of flat colors and represent several legends, such as Perseus bearing off Medusa's head; Orion, the hunter, carrying his catch, the Gorgon's head; and the daughters of Proitos, king of Tiryns.

Again, near Volos in Thessaly painted marble gravestones (*stelai*) have been found, good run-of-the-mill examples of their period, commercial productions of the third century B.C. They show an advance in technique. The surviving upper half of one gravestone uses a wider range and a mixture of colors, and tries to give depth to the scene by making persons in the background a little smaller. The picture shows a room in a house with, in the foreground, a young wife lying dead on her couch, her husband (whose head only is to be seen) at its foot, an old woman nursing a child standing beyond the couch, and an older child in the rear peeping in through a half-open door.

*Vase painting*      Masterpieces of miniature painting are, however, to be found on Greek vases, and artists can be judged not from the descriptions of a Pausanias describing a lost picture at Delphi or

96      Athens, but from the artist's own signed work, found perhaps in

a grave and now set before our eyes in a great museum's glass cases. Such examples allow us to appreciate the artistry of potters and painters and to follow the developments of their skills. The scenes again illustrate ancient epic legends or dramatic performances or aspects of daily life. Their findspots, if known, can tell us of the complexities of trade and cultural influences, or date a building or a grave.

An amazing example of the potter's craft by some unknown master of the seventh century B.C. was found in 1961 on Mykonos, not by a professional excavator but by a villager who found its fragments in digging foundations for his house. He collected the pieces, but perhaps fearing delay in his work took no steps to report them. Then a young American archaeologist lodging at his house came across some intriguing molded fragments, wrapped in old newspapers, and took them to the museum. From the fragments the museum technicians rebuilt a great amphora well over a meter high, with fretwork handles and relief scenes on body and neck. They are scenes of the Trojan War, having the vigor and naïve directness of child art. The

*Archaic amphora from Mykonos*

A molded amphora from Mykonos. Relief decoration showing the Trojan Horse and scenes from the Sack of Troy (700–650 B.C.).

97

Signed pots and master painters. *Left:* amphora signed by Exekias as potter and painter, showing Achilles and Ajax at play (*ca.* 550–540 B.C.). *Right:* a detail from an amphora by Amasis (*ca.* 540 B.C.) showing his signature as potter set besides Poseidon; a stand signed by Ergotimos as potter (*ca.* 570–550 B.C.).

(*opposite*) The Kleophon Painter: *stamnos* and sherds. *Stamnos* showing warrior drinking a farewell cup before leaving home and family (*ca.* 430 B.C.). *Below:* large sherd, from a pot by the same painter found near Phidias' workshop at Olympia; smaller sherd, from a bell-*krater* found in an Attic house, showing a maenad painted in a style very near the Kleophon Painter's (detail of next illustration).

main scene on the neck shows the Trojan horse with wheels or rollers beneath its hoofs and seven windows or trapdoors in its sides, each revealing the head of a warrior while others with helmets and bucklers have already emerged. The panels on the body show various scenes of slaughter, and particular incidents mentioned by Homer can be picked out.

*Known vase painters*

Painted pots were often signed. One example will illustrate the black-figured Attic style of the mid-sixth century. The words *Exekias egraphse kapoiese me* ("Exekias decorated and made me") identify the potter and decorator as the same man, and a

comparison with other pots helps date this example to about
550–540 B.C. The decoration on this again shows Homeric
heroes who are identified by their names, written above their
heads, as Achilles and Ajax. They are peacefully occupied for
once, seated before a gaming table. Their equipment differs in
detail from that on the Mykonos amphora and belongs more to
the painter's own day: Corinthian helmets, linen or leather jer-
kins, and, interestingly enough, arm and thigh pieces as well as
greaves, and two throwing spears each.

When a master is thus recognized by name, scholars can
begin to collect his work and attribute to him even unsigned
vases from the peculiarities of his style. On some pots, however,   99

the signature may say only that the person made (*epoiese*) not painted (*egraphse*) that pot. So we have Amasis, a contemporary of Exekias, who signed at least eight pots as potter only; their anonymous painter is conventionally known as the Amasis Painter, and many more pots are credited to him on grounds of style. It was he who painted the well-known lekythos, or oil flask, with the vivid scenes of women carding and weaving wool. Or again, the scholar may be able to pick out the work of some anonymous hand and may name the painter after a museum where a masterpiece of his is kept, after a subject chosen by him, or after a name inscribed on one of his vases. So we have such names of convenience as the Berlin Painter, the Florence Painter, and the Chicago Painter, and the Achilles Painter, Perseus Painter, Painter of Woolly Satyrs, and again the Kleophon Painter.

*Kleophon Painter*  The Kleophon Painter is named after the words *Kleophon kalos kalos* ("lovely, lovely Kleophon") written on a *stamnos* now kept in the Leningrad collection in Russia. Other works by the same hand have been recognized. They belong to the red-figured period of the fifth century B.C.; the background is painted in with black glaze, the subjects left in the red of the baked clay, and the details indicated with black lines. His pots are usually of the larger kind; bowls, jars, and pitchers —*amphorae, kraters, pelikai, hydriai,* and *stamnoi.* The scenes are often connected with the worship of Dionysus and show sacrifices, worshipers, satyrs, maenads (women in religious frenzy), and banquet scenes. An example found in Italy and now in Copenhagen shows on one side a satyr and maenads, and on the other a chorus of men, a flute player, and a poet identified by name as Phrynicus, an Athenian comedy writer who produced his plays between 434 and 405 B.C. Another example, here illustrated, a *stamnos* from Vulci in Italy and now at Munich in Germany, depicts a warrior taking leave of his wife and parents and drinking a farewell cup. A pot with an identical scene by the same hand is now in Leningrad. In general this painter drew very carefully, and his subjects have idealized features, full-bodied figures, and flowing draperies. His painted pots date from about 435 B.C. to the late 420's.

*Potsherds*  The study of such masterpieces by specialists can help the field archaeologist with his problems too, for it will help classify

100  and date the sherds on which he must often rely. In 1959 there

A fine pot, now fragments. Assembled sherds of a bell *krater* recovered from an Attic house near Ano Liosia, with maenad scene to left of handle and banquet scene to right.

was found in Phidias' workshop at Olympia a fragment of a *krater* which can be attributed by style to the Kleophon Painter. A date of about 430 B.C. is suggested for it and that fits in well with what is known of Phidias' career. The great sculptor was busy earlier supervising the building of the Parthenon (which went on from 447 to 432 B.C.). He finished his gold and ivory Athena for the temple in 438, was exiled from Athens for political reasons later on, and so probably reached Olympia about 430 B.C.

In 1960, when Hugh, John, and I excavated a country house north of Athens, near Ano Liosia, we too collected several fragments of a bell *krater*, once no doubt one of the few best pieces of that household but found smashed and scattered on the floor of the court and rooms. Photographs shown by us to experts in the field, Dr. Lullies of Munich and Sir John Beazley of Oxford, drew from them the opinion that these worn fragments were in a style very near the Kleophon Painter's. The painted *krater* had on one side a banquet scene with four men on couches and a girl flute player, and on the other a Dionysiac scene with a maenad. A general date of 440–420 B.C. suggested by Beazley for the *krater* fixes the general period of the house. As that lay right on the road taken by the Spartan army in its destructive first invasion of Attica, the start of almost thirty years of warfare between Athens and Sparta (the Peloponnesian War,

431–403 B.C.), one could imagine the wine bowl being smashed and the building destroyed on the selfsame day in the spring of 431 B.C. However, the rather later appearance of other sherds, belonging to pots with probably shorter useful lives, suggests that the house was erected in the seven-year interval (421–413 B.C.) between two hot-war phases of the conflict and that both house and pots were destroyed when invasions recommenced.

*Ostraka*     The pots so far mentioned were useful to the ancient Greeks when whole, and after breaking were usually thrown away or just left lying about. As potsherds, they have some value for us. The ancient Greeks made one final use of at least some potsherds as a kind of voting ticket, and these have even greater value for us. They are now called *ostraka,* the Greek word for "seashells" or "potsherds," since it was on an *ostrakon* (in the sense of "sherd," of course, not "shell") that the individual Athenian citizen wrote the name of the politician whom he voted to send into exile—to ostracize—as a man dangerous to the city's democratic way of life. It was one of the citizen's safeguards against tyranny that he could opt each year to hold a special meeting in the Agora and hold a ballot to send one man away for ten years, the victim being the one with the most votes, in a total vote of at least 6,000. The right to ostracize was not used every single year and was in fact exercised only for 70 years in the fifth century, the first occasion being in 487 when Hipparchus (a relative of the old tyrant Hippias who had attempted a return to power with Persian help in 490) was exiled. Ostracism was soon made into a political weapon in the rivalry between factions and pressure groups, and was blatantly used in 417, or shortly after, against the popularist leader Hyperbolus; after that it was never used again.

Once inscribed and used, the *ostraka* were dumped. Several thousand have been recovered in the Agora by Americans and in the nearby Ceramicus cemetery by Germans. The sherds, with names scratched or painted on them, tell us much about various sides of life. They show how literate the ordinary citizen might be, how Ionian alphabet forms of certain letters replaced the Attic forms, how certain names (known to us as spelled in more formal texts) sounded to the ear of the ordinary man. They show how a campaign was mounted against an individual: one large hoard was of ballots against Themistocles (ostracized about 470 B.C.), very many written by the same hand, prepared

102

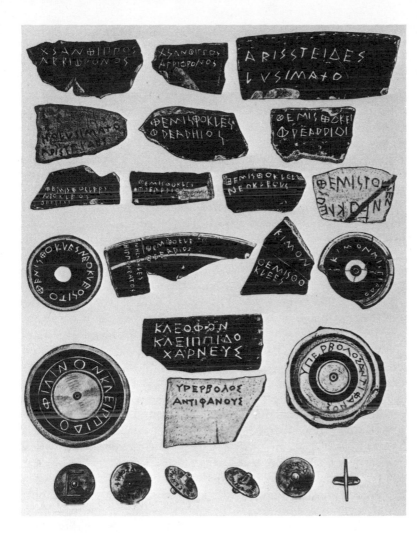

*Ostraka* and jury ballots.
*Row 1*—
Xanthippus, son of Arriphron; Aristeides, son of Lysimachus.
*Row 2*—
Lysimachus' Aristeides; Themistocles of Phraerrhia.
*Row 3*—
Themistocles, son of Neocles and of Phraerrhia.
*Row 4*—
Themistocles; Megakles, son of Hippocrates; Cimon, son of Miltiades.
*Row 5*—
Philinon and Kleophon, sons of Kleippides; Hyperbolus, son of Antiphon.
*Row 6*—
Jury ballots, hollow hubs to left, solid to right.

beforehand for quick distribution to voters. They bring before us the names of many famous men, some whose exile can be dated: Megacles (486), Xanthippus, Pericles' father (484), Aristides (482), Cimon (461), and Pericles. They show again how of the Athenian's three names—his personal name, his father's (patronymic), and his deme's (demotic)—the personal and patronymic were generally applied to men of aristocratic or established families; so Cimon is always "son of Miltiades" and 103

Aristides always "son of Lysimachos." But men with less pretensions or those who stressed the common touch were very often known by their name and demotic: Themistocles is usually "of Phrearria."

Sometimes the *ostraka* revive for us the names of otherwise unknown politicians. Sometimes they give details about those already familiar to us from literature but not by their full names. These they have given to a certain Kleophon, who was known only as a popular spokesman in the 15 years or so before his death in 404 B.C., a man lampooned by the comic poets who never mention his family but only his trade and his vulgarity. Through the *ostraka,* Kleophon is no longer a nobody, but known to have been the son of Kleippides (general in 429–428 B.C.) of the deme Acharnai, and brother of Philinos, son of Kleippides, who was also named on some *ostraka*—and no wonder, if he were the same as the Philinos known to have been condemned round about this time for embezzling public money!

Ostracism was a device adopted elsewhere in Greece, at Megara and at Argos. What may be called petalism existed at Syracuse, for there the intended victim's name was written on *petala*, "olive leaves." These are unlikely to leave any traces for the archaeologist. Hard evidence for a different kind of voting ballot comes again from Athens. In a corner of the Agora, in a building which might have been an open-air court, there was found a container formed of two tiles set up on end, making a simple kind of box. In it were found a few metallic disks with a central spindle or axle, some solid, some tubular. One of each kind was issued to each member of the mass juries of the popular courts, and, in giving his verdict, the juror filed past the box, dropping in one ballot and discarding the other in another place. The solid hub stood for "not guilty," the hollow for "guilty" ; the ends would be hidden by the fingers to ensure secrecy.

*Jury court ballots*

These ballots, like the potsherds, may not seem very impressive, but such small finds, the bric-à-brac of ancient life and of excavations, collected singly or in bagfuls have added a great deal to our understanding of all sites.

# CHAPTER SIX

# Sites Worth Seeing

One of the archaeologist's best guides to Greek sites is the ancient travel book *Periegesis tes Hellados* ("A Tour of Greece") written by that unwearying traveler Pausanias, sometime about A.D. 150–60. Pausanias was particularly interested in antiquities, and by his day classical buildings and statues would already be ancient monuments. He described very many that impressed him, and his final comment was often *theas axia*—"worth seeing."

Let us follow the advice of Pausanias and visit a few famous sites, only too few in this short tour, and note what has survived since ancient times and how successful archaeologists have been in revealing and understanding the remains. I say "visit" in the hope that, if at the moment you can only read about them, someday you may see them for yourselves.

We shall start, as did Pausanias, with Athens, the cultural *Athens* capital of Greece for a very long time in antiquity and now of course the political capital. Athens in the fifth century B.C. was much smaller than the great and still-growing city which you will see nowadays. Its vast tracts of suburbs were once open countryside dotted with hamlets and homesteads, and this home plain of Athens provided very many of its citizens with work and with food. Ancient Athens "just grew" and so, unlike Olynthus, its street plan was irregular. It was encircled with defensive walls. So also was the harbor city of Piraeus, but Hippodamus was brought in to give the fast-growing town a fashionable grid plan. For over 50 years in the fifth century B.C. (458–404 B.C.) and again in the fourth (from 393 B.C. on), the two cities were linked by Long Walls, creating a safe corridor between them.

The most ancient as well as the most imposing part of Athens *Acropolis* was the Acropolis, the "High City." This is a long rock rising like a battleship out of the sea of houses that surrounds it. It was 105

The Acropolis of Athens: reconstruction view. View as from northwest, with Mt. Hymettus in the background.

a citadel fortified at a very early date, and its fortifications have undergone alterations and attacks at various times over 3,000 years and more, on occasions long forgotten and occasions still famous.

The great rock has been the center of archaeological activity ever since men became interested in antiquarian studies, and the earliest excavations of the newly independent Greek state in 1833 were directed to renewing its ancient glories. It has been dug down to solid rock over a good deal of its area, and for many years now work has been confined to conservation, discreet restoration, and restudy of its wonderful architecture and sculpture.

The Acropolis in its present state is stripped of almost everything but the remains of its classical buildings. It appears now as a plateau, with a gentle slope to the west, standing over 70 meters above the plain and measuring some 300 meters long and 140 meters wide over its present walls. The latter, although in places refaced and buttressed with medieval and Turkish additions, represent mainly the rebuilding and extension of the citadel defences by Themistocles and Cimon, son of Miltiades, in the fifth century B.C. The straight lengths of wall on the east and south sides give a false impression of regularity to the hill; for they were erected well in front of the natural crests of the rock and the spaces behind were filled in, largely with the debris of buildings sacked by the Persians in 480 B.C. (a fertile source of finds to the excavators of the 1880's). In this way great terraces were built up, enlarging the area available for temple building. There had been earlier defenses, Mycenaean walls of the rougher boulder construction called Cyclopean work (being credited to the giants or Cyclopes). These, following the contours more closely, were for the most part buried under the later extensions—where archaeologists have traced their course—but in places left exposed, as at the western end near the great entrance.

The easiest approach is from the west along the saddle between the Areopagus, or "Hill of Ares," and the Acropolis. Nowadays we pass through a gate on the south side, entering the sloping area between the fifth-century colonnaded Propylaea ("Foregate") and the Roman gateway, the Beulé Gate (so called after the French scholar who cleared it in 1853). On our right is a rectangular tower, thrust forward to protect the south side of the approach and to threaten us, if we were ancient attackers, with counterfire on our unshielded (right) sides. However, the bastion is crowned with nothing more dangerous than the elegant white marble temple of Nike ("Victory"), a small building some 9 meters in length with a graceful four-column Ionic porch in front of its open east end, and a similar false porch at the west. It represents part of a great scheme to beautify the Acropolis with temples and fine monuments, and dates to 427–424 B.C. Military needs were reemphasized when the Turks in 1687 dismantled the temple to mount a battery on its site. From the scattered blocks it was rebuilt, not too accurately, in 1835 by the Bavarian architects Ross, Schaubert, and Hansen. Then in 1935–40 it was taken apart and correctly rebuilt by Professor A. K. Orlandos, now secretary general of the Archaeological Society and one of the experts in the reconstruction of antiquities. This latest work revealed also that the classical

*Temple of Victory*

107

squared masonry of the bastion was a casing for a Mycenaean outflanking bastion.

There are still some traces of postclassical work near the Propylaea. One is a 4-meter-high limestone and marble pedestal of a statue erected about 27–12 B.C. to M. Vipsanius Agrippa, general of the first Roman emperor, Augustus. Another is a great Roman staircase that replaced the zigzag approach way. Most of the medieval and later walls that had turned this western end of the rock into a great castle were removed by Kyriakos Pittakis (who was the first Greek to be conservator of antiquities), by Beulé and others. Schliemann financed the removal of a lofty "Frankish" tower by the Archaeological Society in 1875.

*Propylaea*  The Propylaea was built as a double porch, facing east and west, with Doric external columns and Ionic internal ones, and there are forward-jutting wings with Doric columns facing inward onto the front porch. The north wing is deep and contained paintings by ancient masters, but the south wing does not go so far back, being limited by a 17-meter length of Mycenaean wall left in place, running obliquely to the edge of the Acropolis.

On the Acropolis there are three great buildings, ruined but still standing, all classical and all part of a great building program conceived by Pericles, the famous Athenian statesman, in 447 B.C. or earlier and continued after his death in 429 B.C., until near the end of the century. These are the Propylaea, the Parthenon, and the Erechtheum. The first was designed by Mnesicles and built about 437–432 B.C. It seems that the design was not fully completed, nor again was the finish of the part built; the wall stones retain the lugs (called ears) by which they were raised into position.

*Parthenon*  The Parthenon was built in 447–438 B.C., with work on the sculpture of the pediments continuing until 432. Phidias was general designer, and Ictinus and Callicrates were architects. The material used for this and the other buildings was Pentelic marble, quarried from a mountain northeast of Athens. The temple was one of the largest Doric temples on the Greek mainland; it was nearly 70 meters long and 31 meters wide on its top step, or stylobate. Its peristyle, or all-round colonnade, had eight columns at the ends and seventeen along the sides (corner columns being counted twice), and each column was over 10 meters high and nearly 2 meters thick at base. The columns were subtly swollen toward the middle and inclined very slightly inward—all refinements intended to overcome the optical illusions arising from the use of straight lines, namely that columns would appear too thin at the middle and outward-leaning at the top. The inner building had two parts. A front porch (*pronaos*) of six columns linked with bronze grilles or lattice screens led into the main cella, exactly 100 ancient Attic feet long. Inside were two-tiered colonnades enclosing the great cult statue of Athena in gold and ivory at its far end. A rear porch (*opisthodomos*) opened into a squarish chamber with four Ionic columns. This was the treasury, which originally bore the name Parthenon, later applied to the temple as a whole. The upper work, including ceiling blocks and tiles, had been of marble. Some of the sculpture remains in place in the pediments, the metopes over the outer colonnades, and the frieze round the inner building; the rest of the surviving parts are to be viewed in the British Museum in London.

Clearance work in and around the Parthenon in the 1830's and later revealed the foundations of yet earlier temples of Athena. One was an "earlier Parthenon," its foundations reused in the base of the Periclean temple. Unfinished, it was destroyed by the Persians in 480 B.C., and some of its column drums were built into the north wall of the Acropolis by Themistocles as a war memorial. An even earlier archaic temple, the Hekatompedon, or "Hundred-footer," had stood on the same site; to it probably belonged some of the archaic limestone sculpture now in the Acropolis museum at the east end of the citadel.

North of the Parthenon are to be seen the foundations of a Doric temple of sixth-century date, attributed to the tyrant Pisistratus and recognized by W. Dörpfeld as an archaic peristyle temple. Among the remains are two column bases far older in date; they represent the sole remnants of the Mycenean palace, which Homer referred to in the *Odyssey* as the "strong house of Erechtheus." Just beyond stands the classical Erechtheum, with its caryatid porch and its Ionic columns. The building was first cleared in 1837 and has been repaired and restudied many times since then. Built in 421–406 B.C., it included several shrines under one roof; worth noting are the delicacy of the decoration of the Ionic order and the use of darker gray marble as a background for the white figures of the frieze.

*Erechtheum*

Since the main clearances in the 1830's leading up to the deeper excavations of Kavvadias and Kawerau in the 1880's and 1890's, restoration work has been undertaken or redone by the Archaeological Society under the direction of many scholars, notably by the Greek architect N. Balanos, who worked on the Erechtheum in 1902–9, on the Propylaea in the next decade, on the Parthenon in 1922–33, and started the work in the Nike temple that was finished by Orlandos.

From the south side of the Acropolis rock we can look into the Theater of Dionysus lying at its eastern foot, the oldest theater in Greece but much altered in Hellenistic and Roman times, and, farther to the west, the Odeum of Herodes Atticus, a Roman-type theater built in the A.D. 160's, excavated by the Archaeological Society in 1857–58, and now restored and reused for modern productions of ancient classical plays.

*Agora*　　From the north side of the citadel one looks down into the ancient Agora, or marketplace, a great open area extending between the Acropolis and the built-up streets of the modern city. This is the site of one of the most ambitious and thorough excavation projects in Greece, the uncovering of the heart of ancient Athens. Work has been carried on for 40 years by the American School of Classical Studies, first under T. Leslie Shear (1931–45), then under Professor Homer A. Thompson (1947–67), and recently under T. Leslie Shear, Jr. A great many modern houses were gradually bought up and demolished. The Turkish and Byzantine houses that underlay them, filling the once open square, had to be investigated and recorded, and then the Roman, Hellenistic, classical, archaic, and prehistoric levels were explored in turn. An archaeological zone now extends from the north slopes of the Acropolis and Areopagus as far as the prominent temple of Hephaestus and the modern railway line, which till lately had defined the north edge of the excavation, but lies south of that of the ancient Agora itself. Most of the area has now been landscaped; bushes have been planted, for example, in the very pits where trees and potted shrubs had been planted in antiquity around Hephaestus' temple. The finds have been exhibited or stored in the rebuilt Stoa of Attalus which closes the Agora on its eastern side, serving both as a museum and as a magnificent sample of Hellenistic architecture. These buildings and finds will fill several volumes in the great Agora series of reports, but glimpses of the tremendous range of information collected can be seen in the attractive *Agora Picture*

*Books.*

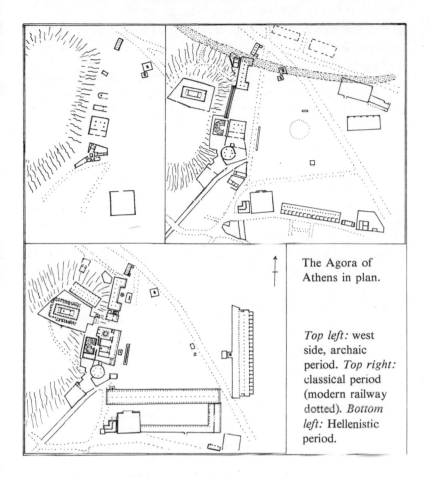

The Agora of
Athens in plan.

*Top left:* west
side, archaic
period. *Top right:*
classical period
(modern railway
dotted). *Bottom
left:* Hellenistic
period.

The history of the site is too complex, the number of buildings
too great, to describe fully here. Plans and sketches will suggest
the general development of the site. In prehistoric times the area
was used as a cemetery with many rock-cut chamber tombs and
then in part as a potters' quarter (hence the name Ceramicus
given to it by Pausanias). But from some time in the seventh or
early sixth century B.C. it was developed as a great public square,
for markets, political assemblies, and the earliest dramatic festi-
vals. Its boundaries were defined at street corners by upright
stones inscribed with a formula, such as *horos eimi tes agoras*
("I am the boundary of the agora").

The earliest archaic civic buildings stood on the west side, in   111

*Civic buildings*  an arc at the foot of the Colonus hill. They included an irregular colonnaded building at the south end, perhaps a magistrates' club; two small buildings later replaced by a square hall where the council met (*bouleuterion*); a small rectangular temple of Meter, mother of the gods; a round-ended temple of Apollo; and a shrine of Zeus. Set farther east at the ends of the arc were an Altar of the Twelve Gods on the north and a large square court, probably the Jury Courts, at the south.

Destroyed by the Persians in 480 B.C., some buildings were repaired, but others, such as the temples of Apollo and Meter, were not replaced till the fourth and second centuries B.C. The fifth century saw several additions: on the west a round building, the tholos, or "officers' mess," for the members of the council's standing committee (*ca.* 470 B.C.); a new Bouleuterion behind the old (*ca.* 420 B.C.); rock-cut steps below the terrace of the temple of Hephaestus (*ca.* 445 B.C.); a winged portico, or Stoa of Zeus (*ca.* 430 B.C.). The south range now comprised the irregular Strategeion ("generals' headquarters"), a fountain house, the square Jury Court, a long colonnade with official dining rooms (*ca.* 420 B.C.), an old fountain house, and a mint. In the fourth century an earlier unfinished public court in the northeast was replaced by a fine peristyle enclosure, and a new temple of Apollo rose on the west.

In the classical period the square was still quite open, crossed only by the processional Sacred Way descending from the Acropolis to the northwest city gates, and going on to Eleusis. But in Hellenistic and Roman times the square became more elaborate, with huge monumental buildings. Several were put up in the second century B.C.: on the west, a new Metroon combining temple and record offices, in place of the old Bouleuterion, and a colonnaded hall alongside the temple of Hephaestus; on the east, the two-storied market hall called the Stoa of Attalus; and on the south, the Middle, East, and new South stoas which turned this end into an almost separate commercial or legal piazza. Roman additions tended to fill up the central area itself, as with the huge Odeum, or "Concert Hall," of Agrippa and the resited temple of Ares. The contrast between the Agora of the age of Pericles and that of Pausanias can best be suggested by reconstruction sketches.

Excavation has not stopped. Rather it has restarted just north of the railway where several buildings, named in ancient records